Texas Tombstones

– New Braunfels –

Tori Sandoval

America
Through
Time

America Through Time®
An imprint of Sutton Publishing Inc.
www.through-time.com

First published 2025

ISBN 978-1-63499-566-5

Typeset in 10pt on 13pt Sabon
Printed and bound in the United States of America

CONTENTS

About the Author

Tori Sandoval, a Texas native, has cultivated her artistic talents across various mediums throughout her life, with a particular passion for digital art and photography. From an early age, Tori has been drawn to the darker, unconventional aspects of creativity, discovering beauty in the unusual. Undeterred by external opinions, she embraced her unique artistic vision and carved out a niche for herself in the art world.

In addition to her work in photography and digital art, Tori enjoys reading, writing, traveling, hiking, indulging in coffee, and sharing laughter and memories with her favorite people: her husband and their two children.

INTRODUCTION

There is a certain stillness in a cemetery that I find both haunting and peaceful. For as long as I can remember, I have been drawn to these sacred spaces, not out of sorrow, but out of curiosity, reverence, and a deep appreciation for history. Cemeteries hold the stories of those who came before us, yet with time, many of these stories begin to fade. Loved ones who once stood beside these graves eventually stop visiting, and over the years, nature takes over. Headstones become weathered, names become unreadable, and entire sections of cemeteries slip into silence and obscurity.

New Braunfels, Texas, is a town deeply rooted in heritage and tradition, founded in 1845 by German settlers seeking a new beginning. Nestled in the Texas Hill Country, it quickly flourished, blending German customs with the rugged beauty of Texas. This unique fusion is still evident today in its historic buildings, festivals, and long-standing traditions. Its cemeteries serve as silent witnesses to this rich past, holding the names of pioneers, families, and forgotten souls who built the town's foundation. Through worn headstones and intricate memorials, their legacy remains etched in stone, waiting to be remembered.

My photography is not just about capturing old headstones or crumbling statues; it is about preserving the memory of those who rest beneath them. As I wander through the cemeteries, I take in the intricate craftsmanship of the headstones, the way the elements have softened their edges, and the quiet mementos left behind. I speak to those laid to rest here, acknowledging their presence so they are not entirely forgotten. I take the time to clear away fallen leaves, straighten a flower arrangement, or wipe away dirt from an inscription, small acts to show that someone still cares.

This book is a collection of moments and memories, a way to honor those who came before us and to capture the beauty in the stillness of time. Through my lens, I invite you to step into these historic cemeteries, to appreciate their artistry, to reflect on their forgotten stories, and to see them not as places of sorrow, but as places of remembrance, history, and quiet reverence.

1
MISTS OF MEMORY

The Foggy Landscape of a New Braunfels Cemetery

In this chapter, we delve into the haunting beauty of a New Braunfels' historic cemetery where nature and memory intertwine in quiet elegance. Most of the images ahead were captured on foggy days, when the mist drapes over weathered headstones and towering oaks, transforming the landscape into a mysterious, ethereal canvas. The soft diffusion of light through the fog lends a surreal quality to each scene, inviting you to pause and reflect on the passage of time and the silent stories etched into stone. As you journey through these pages, let the veil of fog guide you into a world where every shadow, every whisper of nature, celebrates the enduring legacy of those who rest here.

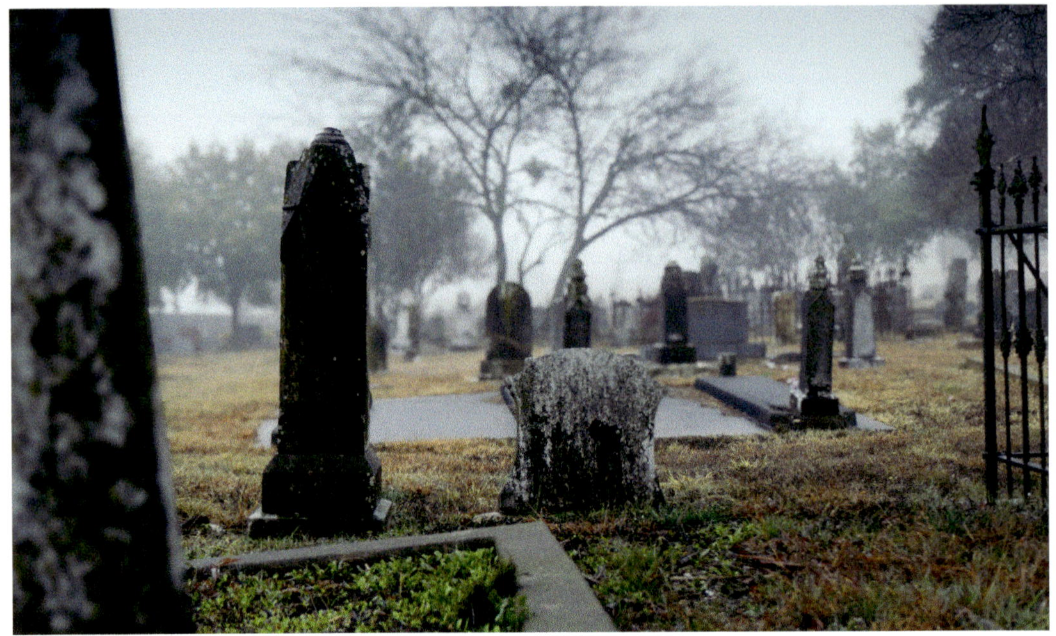

In the gentle morning mist, faded tombstones whisper stories of long-forgotten lives.

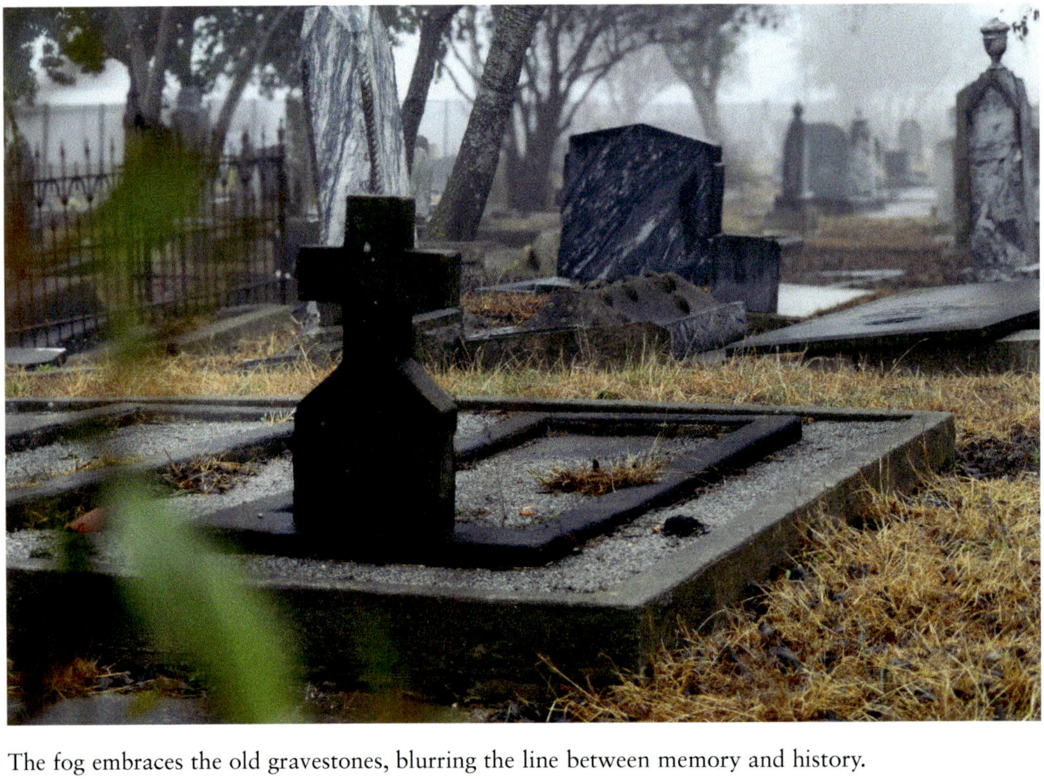

The fog embraces the old gravestones, blurring the line between memory and history.

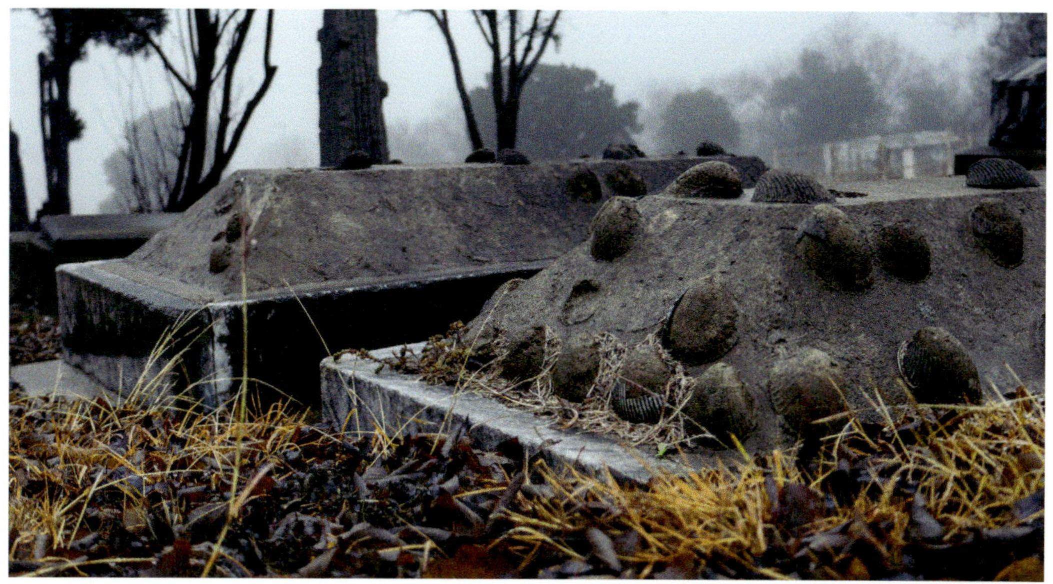

Seashells represent rebirth and resurrection, embodying Christian themes of baptism and the soul's journey to eternal life. In German communities, they symbolize renewal and the hope of life after death.

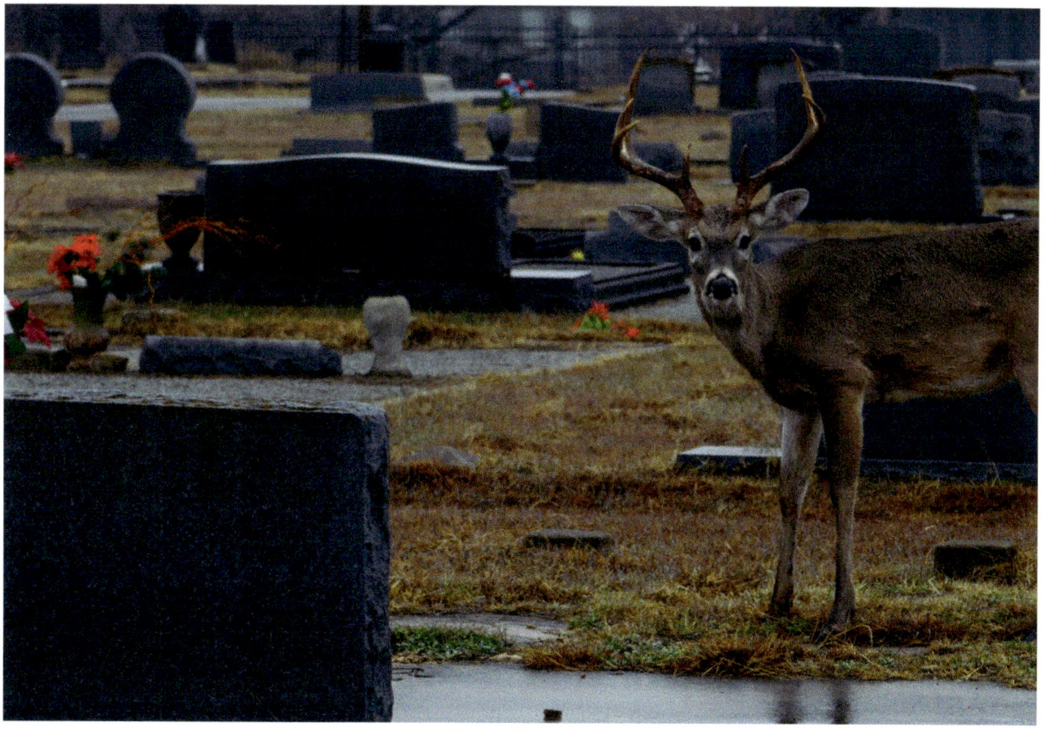

A lone buck stands among the tombstones.

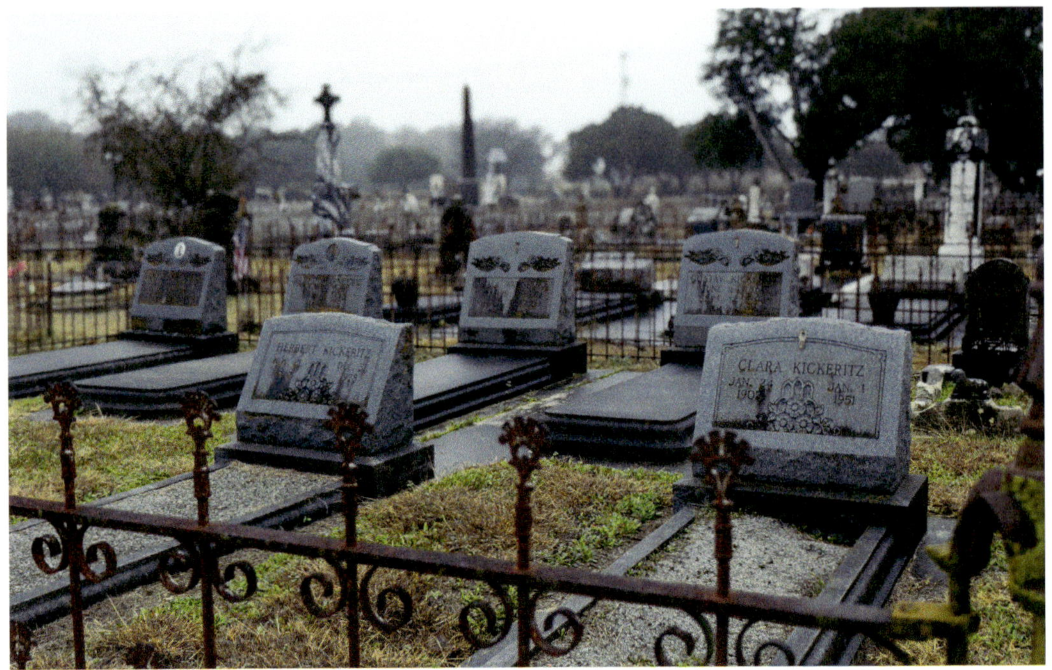

A family burial plot belonging to the Kickeritz family in the Comal Cemetery.

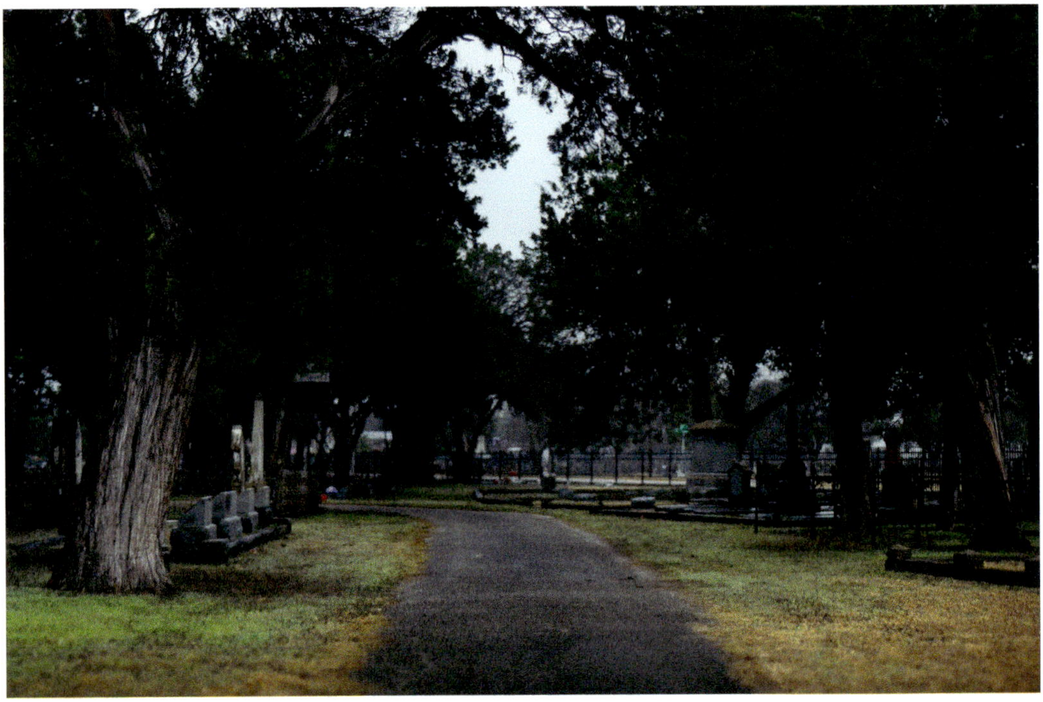

A tree-lined road curves through the cemetery.

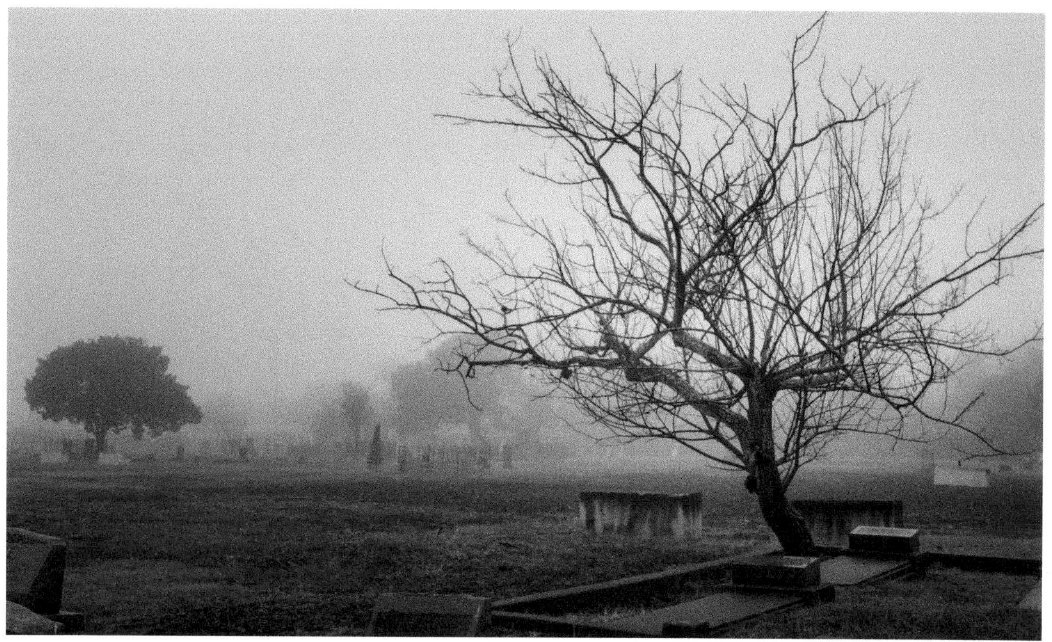

A lone, bare tree stands in the fog, its branches reaching into the silent mist in New Braunfels Cemetery.

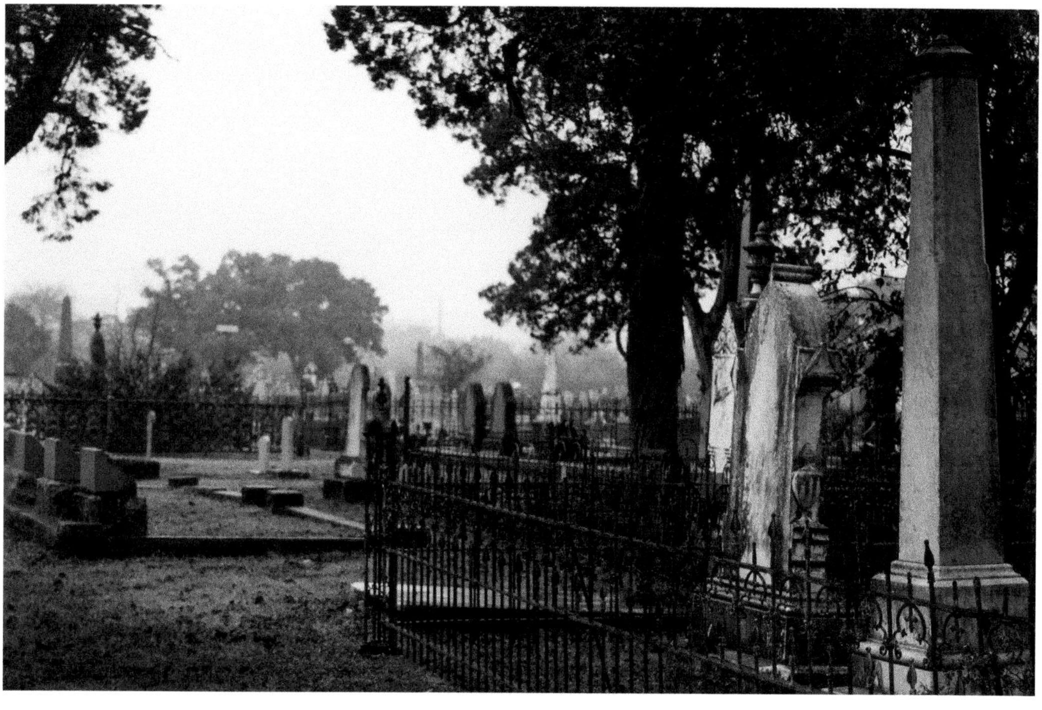

Weathered tombstones stand in the soft stillness of the morning.

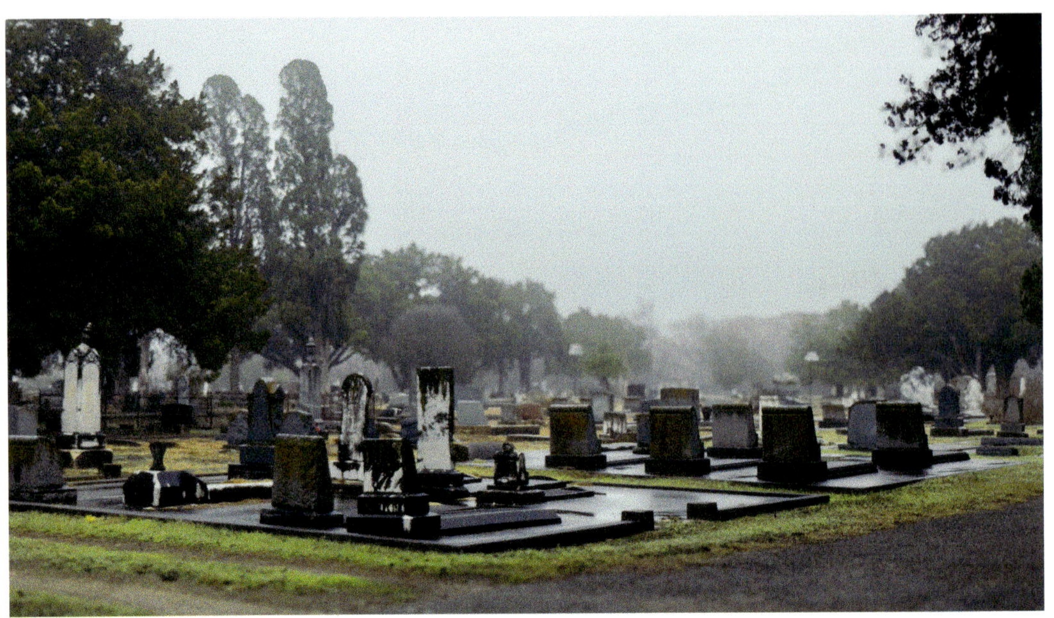

Rows of tombs fade into the soft embrace of the morning fog.

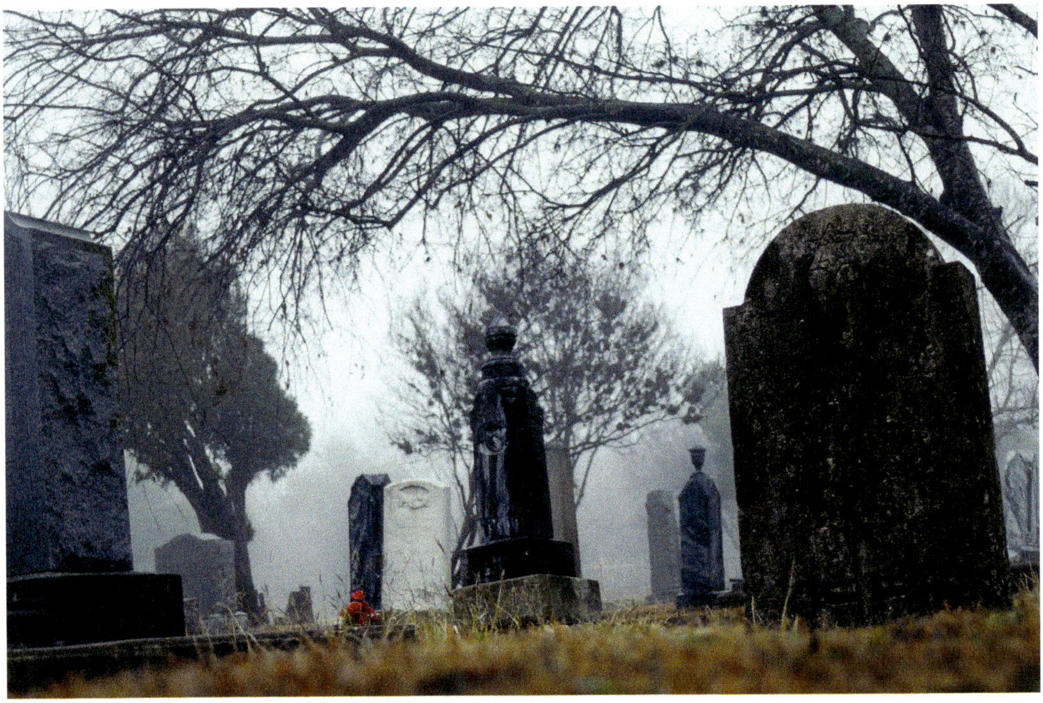

A part of the headstone reads: "Here rests in God." An ancestor of bygone days born in Ibbenbüren, Germany.

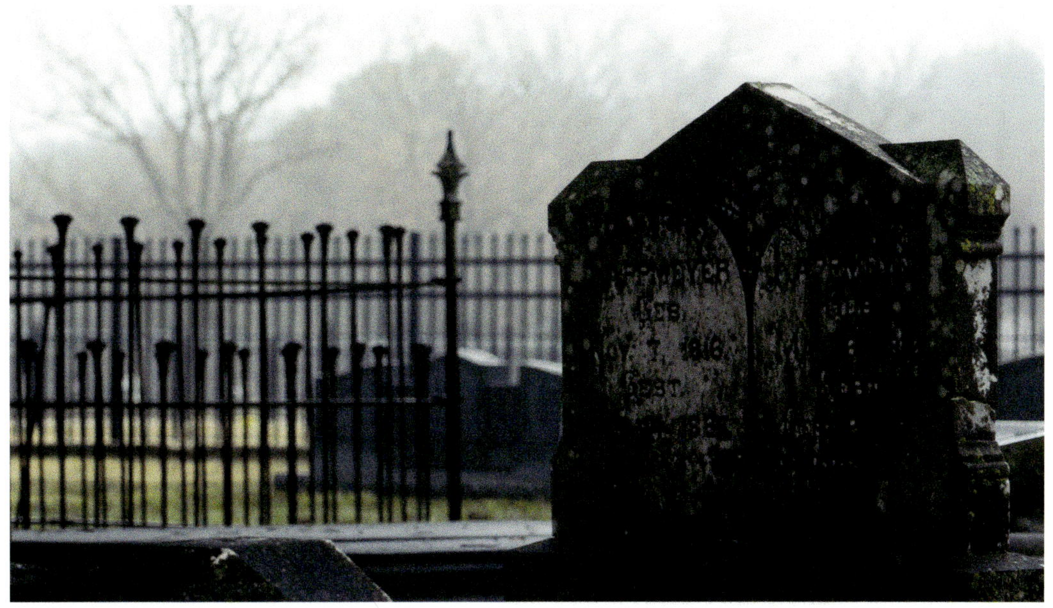

Spouses, Conrad and Wilhelmine Kappmeyer, rest side by side in Comal Cemetery, their legacy etched in stone and memory.

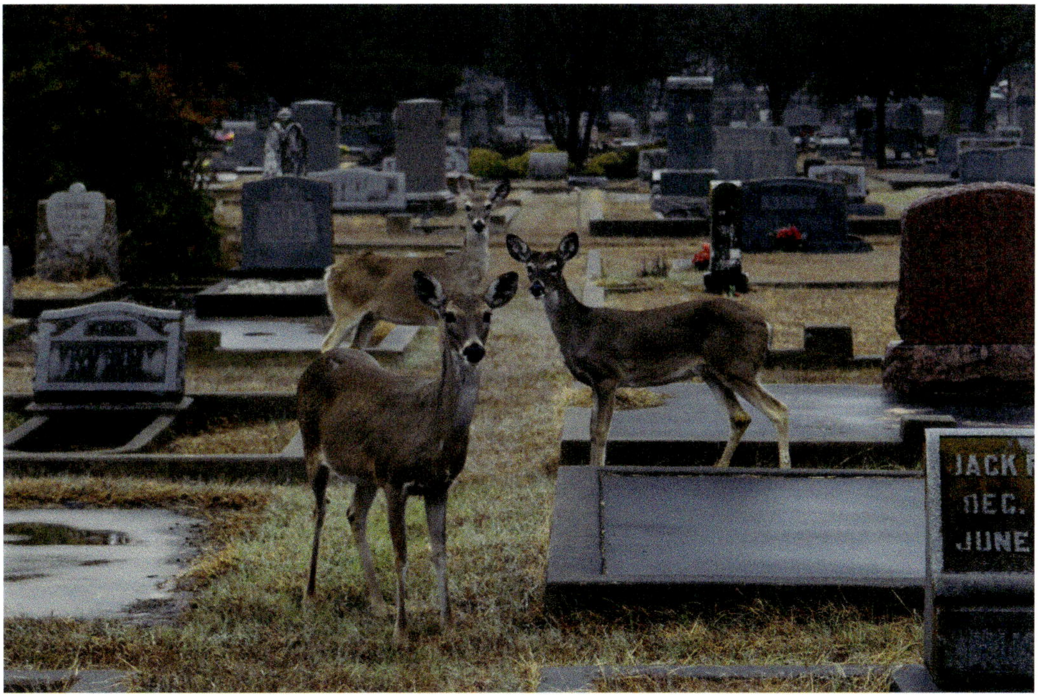

A graceful trio of deer stands silently among the tombstones, blending into the quiet serenity of the cemetery.

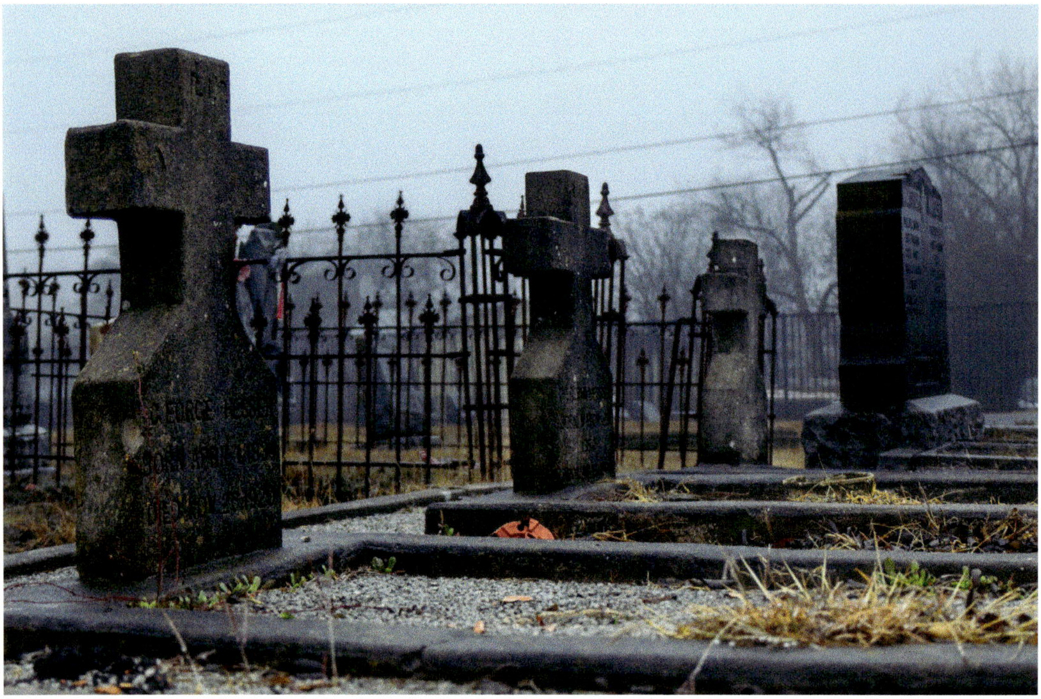

Weathered cross-shaped tombstones stand solemnly against a backdrop of soft, drifting fog.

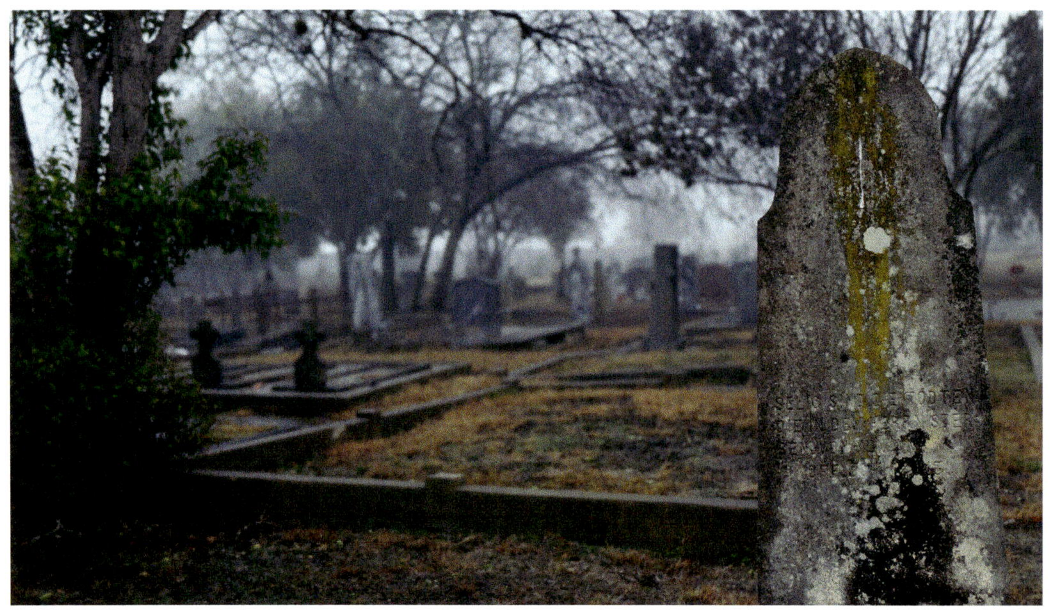

"*Selig sind die Toten, die in dem Herrn sterben von nun an.*" "Blessed are the dead who die in the Lord from now on." A timeless inscription of faith and eternal rest, often found on German gravestones.

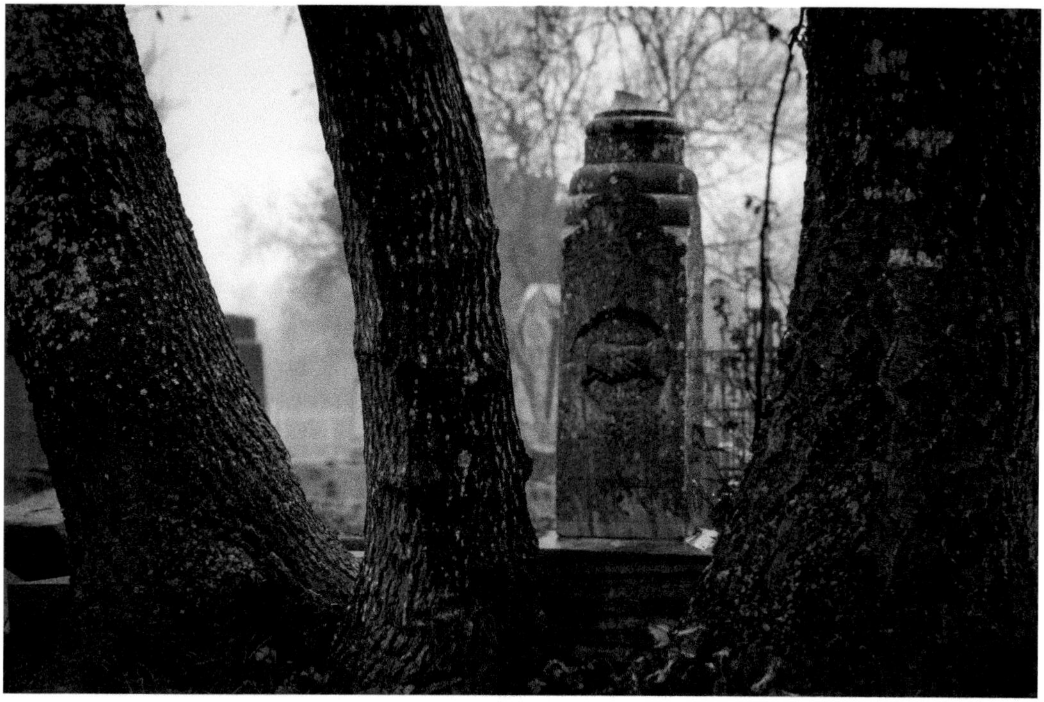

Trees grow around a weathered tombstone, nature reclaiming what was once left in memory.

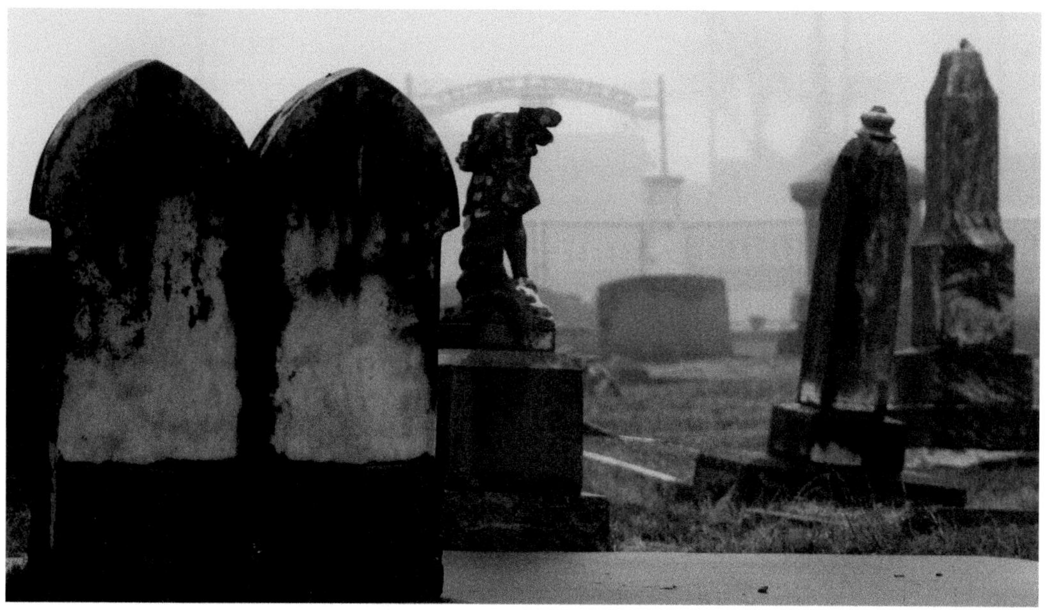

Aging tombstones stand solemnly in the mist, their surfaces worn by time.

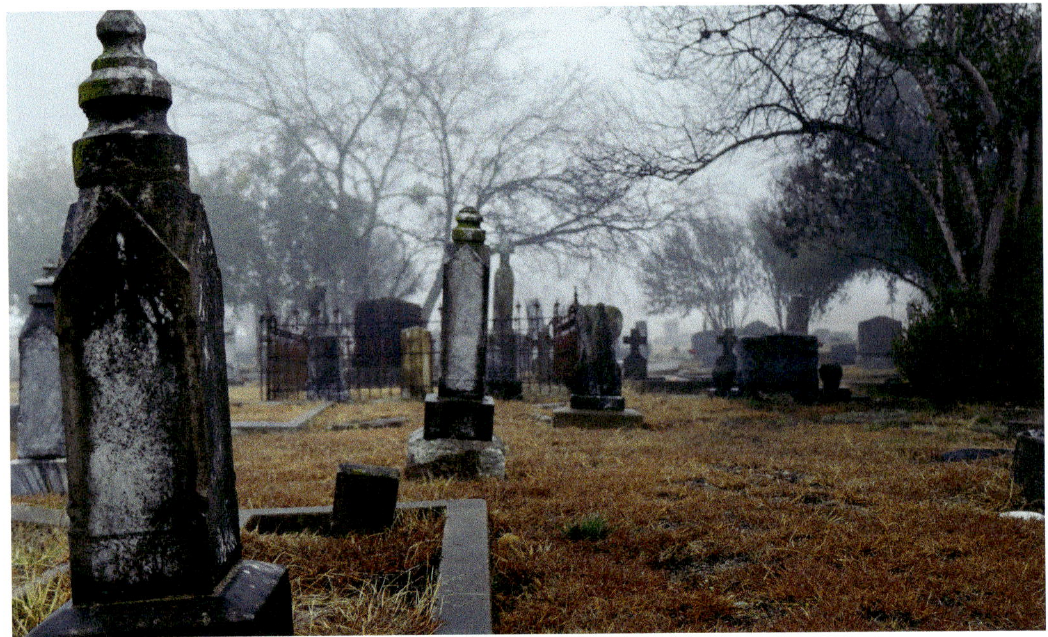

The fog-draped landscape of the cemetery stretches into the distance, where weathered tombstones and bare trees stand as silent reminders of time's passage.

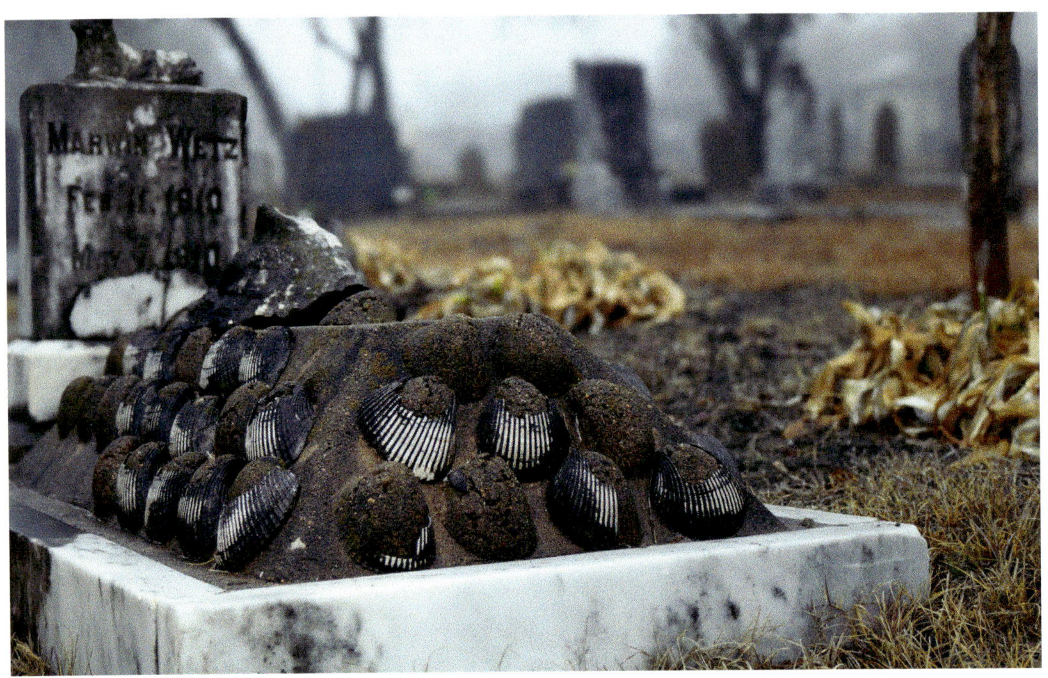

Amid the misty landscape of the cemetery, this unique grave adorned with seashells stands as a quiet tribute, weathered by time yet rich in symbolism and memory.

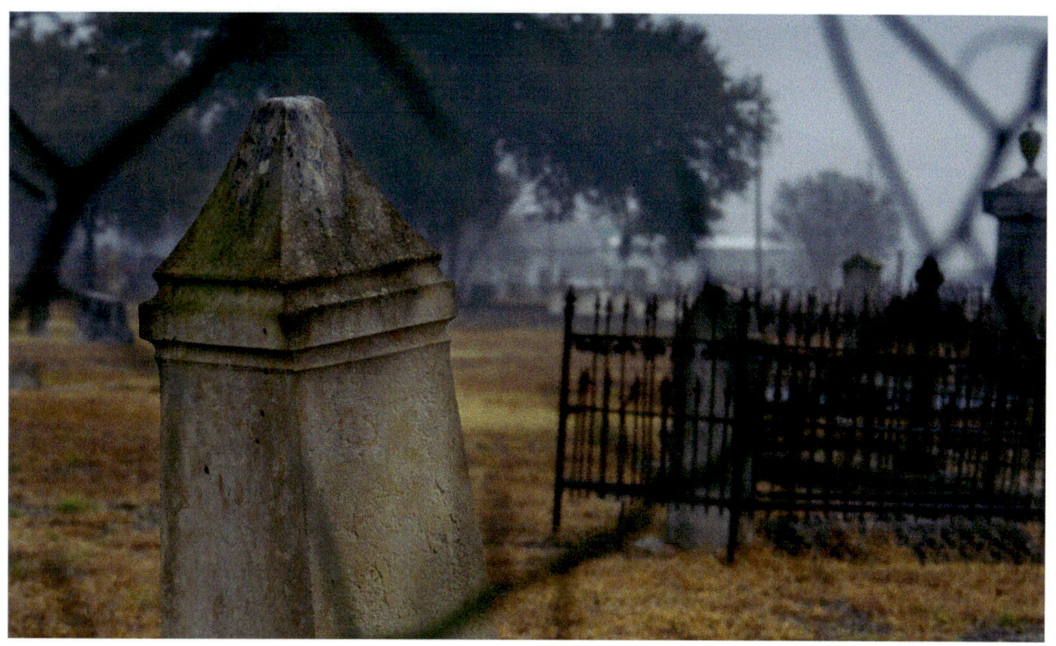

Through the soft haze of fog, a weathered tombstone leans gently within the quiet cemetery landscape, framed by rusted ironwork and towering trees in the distance.

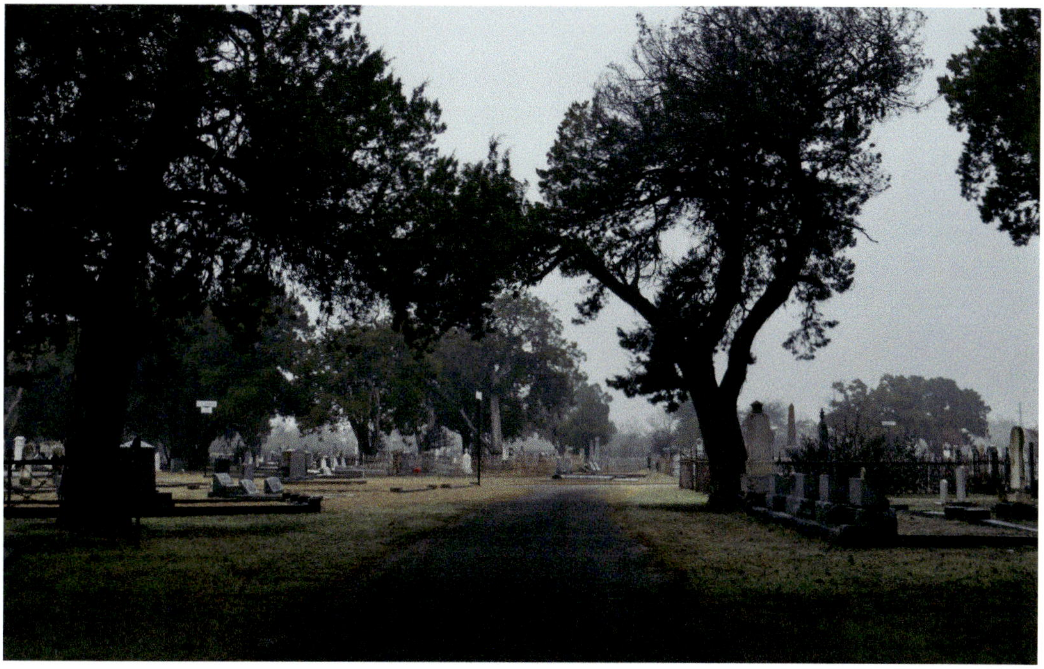

Beyond the quiet, cemetery road, fog lingers in the distance, softening the outlines of aged tombstones and iron fences adding to the solemn beauty of the landscape.

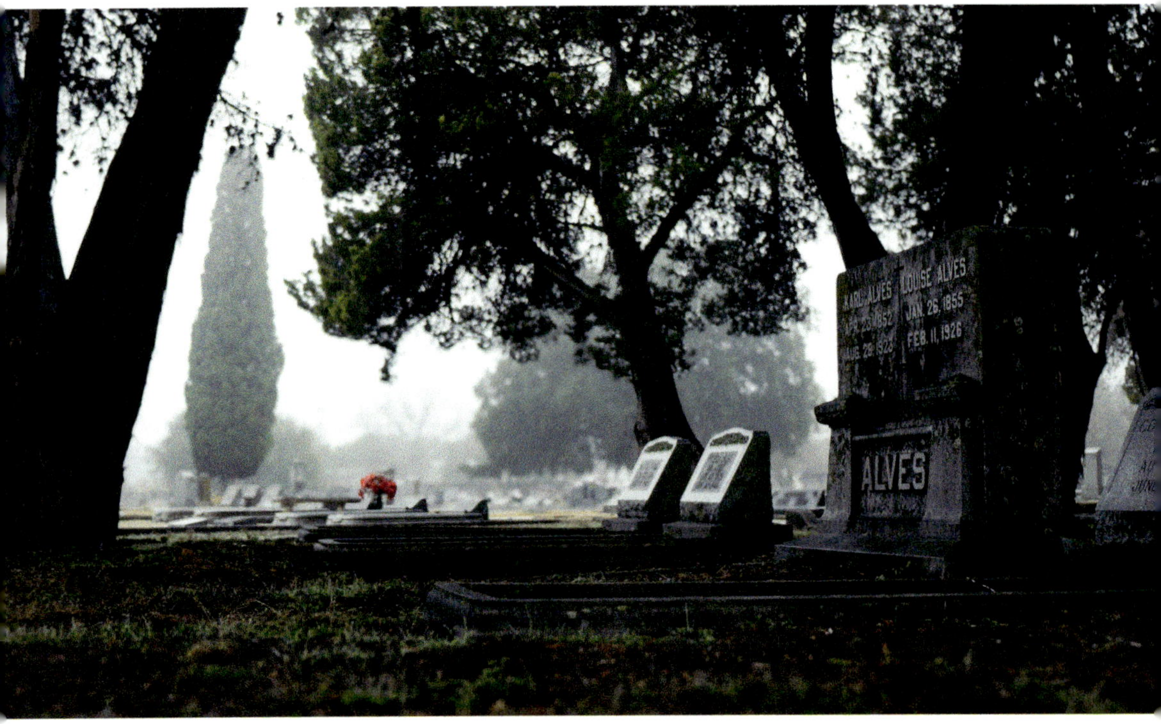
KARL ALVES
LOUISE ALVES
JAN. 26, 1855
FEB. 11, 1926
ALVES

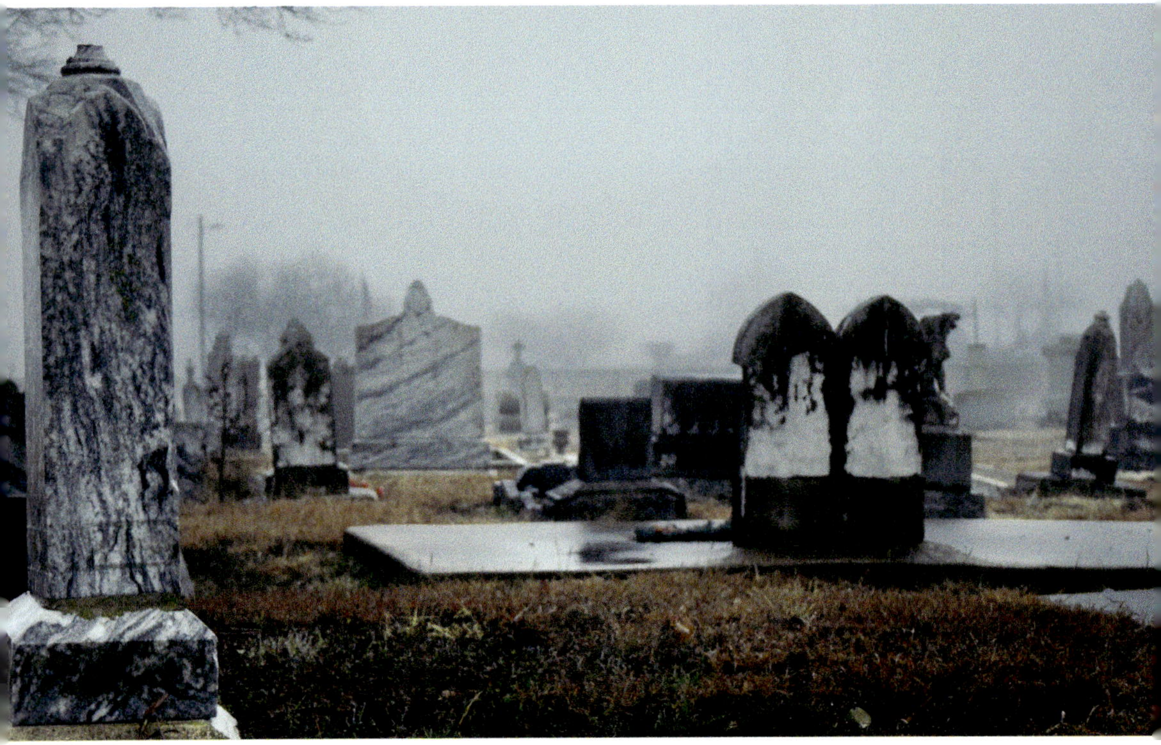

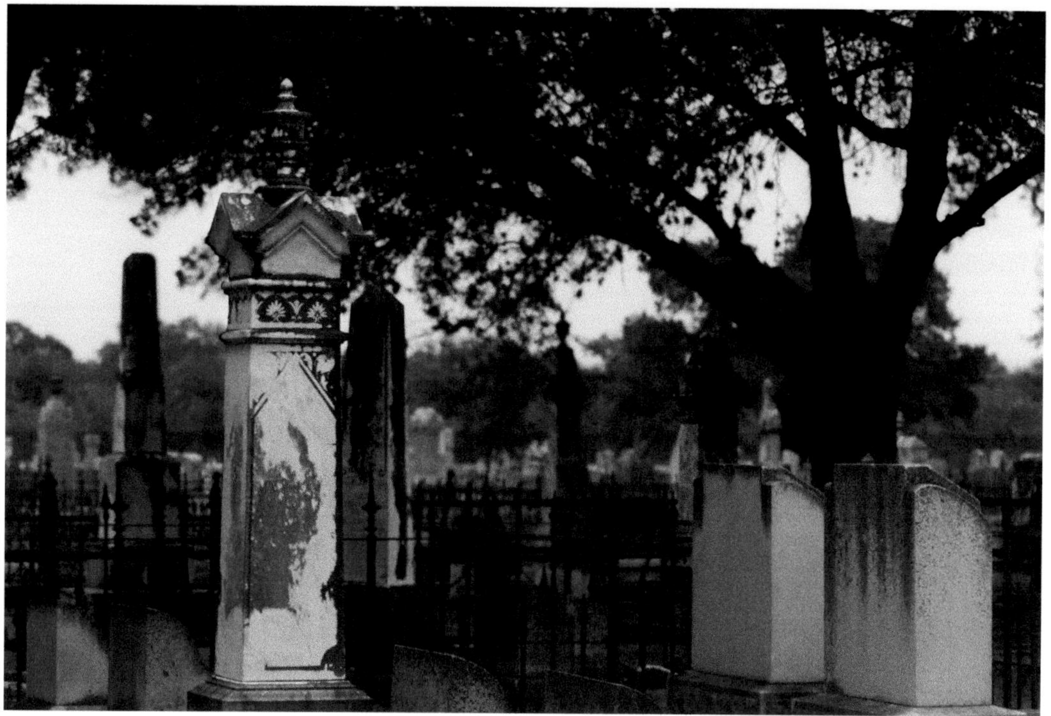

A towering, weathered headstone stands among the rusted iron fences and aging graves.

Opposite above: In Comal Cemetery, a couple's headstone stands as the focal point of this image, framed by towering trees, where they rest beneath the quiet canopy.

Opposite below: The tall marble headstone stands boldly as weathered graves fade into the mist, creating a hauntingly beautiful blend of time and memory.

2
LAMENT IN MARBLE

Stories in the Ruins

Amid the quiet, hallowed grounds of New Braunfels' cemetery, the headstones stand as silent testifiers to lives long past. Once carved with care and precision, these markers have been softened by time. Their faded inscriptions, chipped edges, and weathered surfaces reveal the relentless passage of years. Each headstone bears the gentle scars of decay, yet every crack and blemish speak of enduring stories of love, loss, and memory. In this chapter, we explore these ancient stones. Quiet witnesses to forgotten histories invite us to reflect on life's impermanence and the enduring power of remembrance.

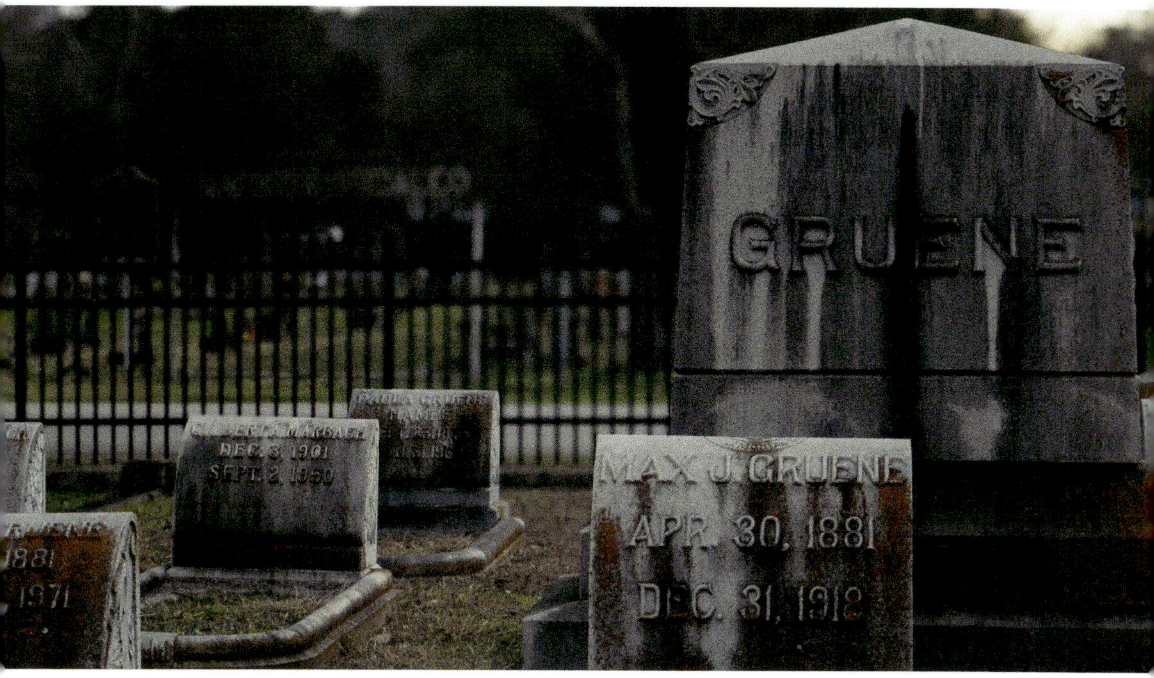

The Gruene family, known for shaping the growth of New Braunfels, Texas, has several members laid to rest in local cemeteries.

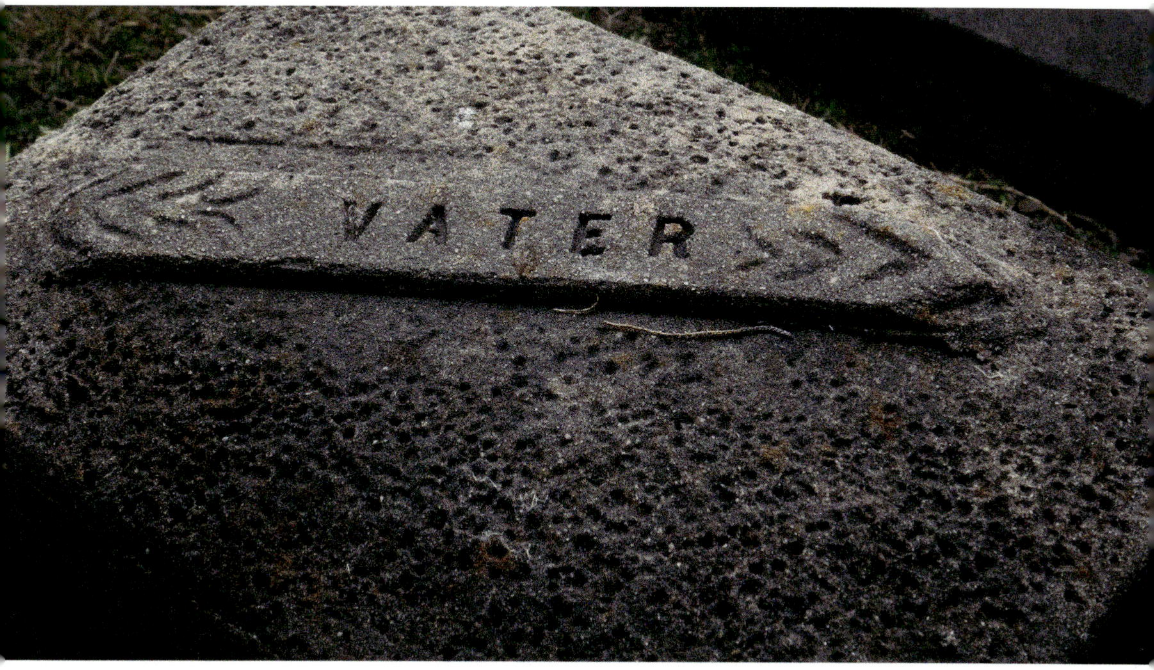

A weathered tombstone inscribed with "Vater" stands as a solemn tribute to a father long remembered.

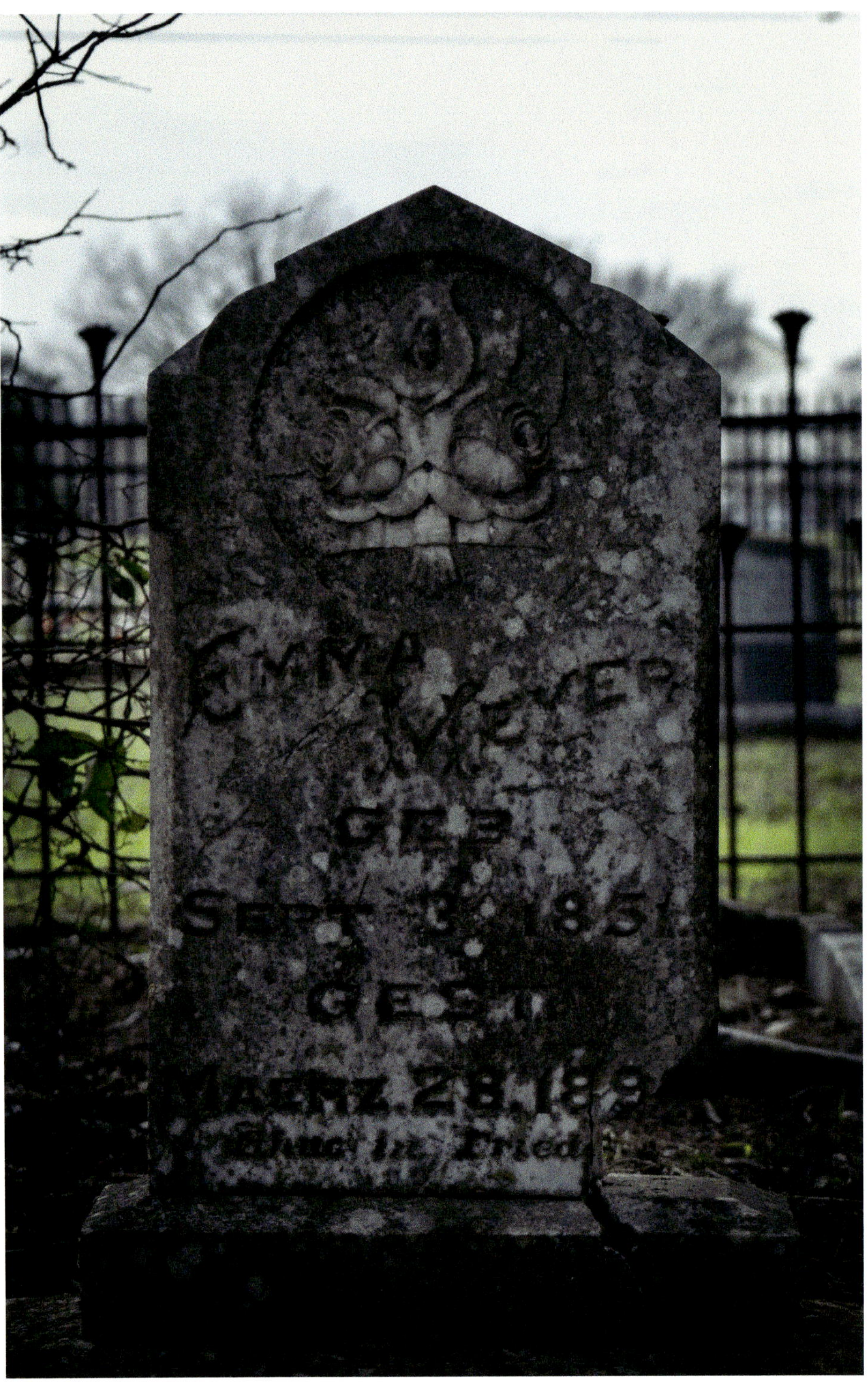

Emma Meyer's worn tombstone, adorned with carved flowers.

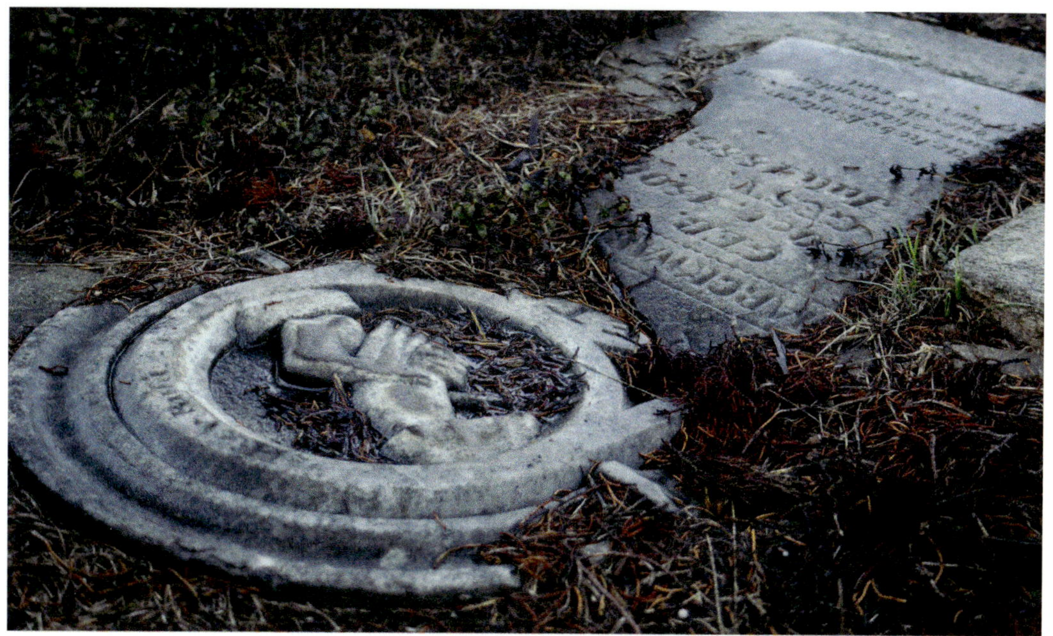

A sunken tomb, slowly reclaimed by the earth.

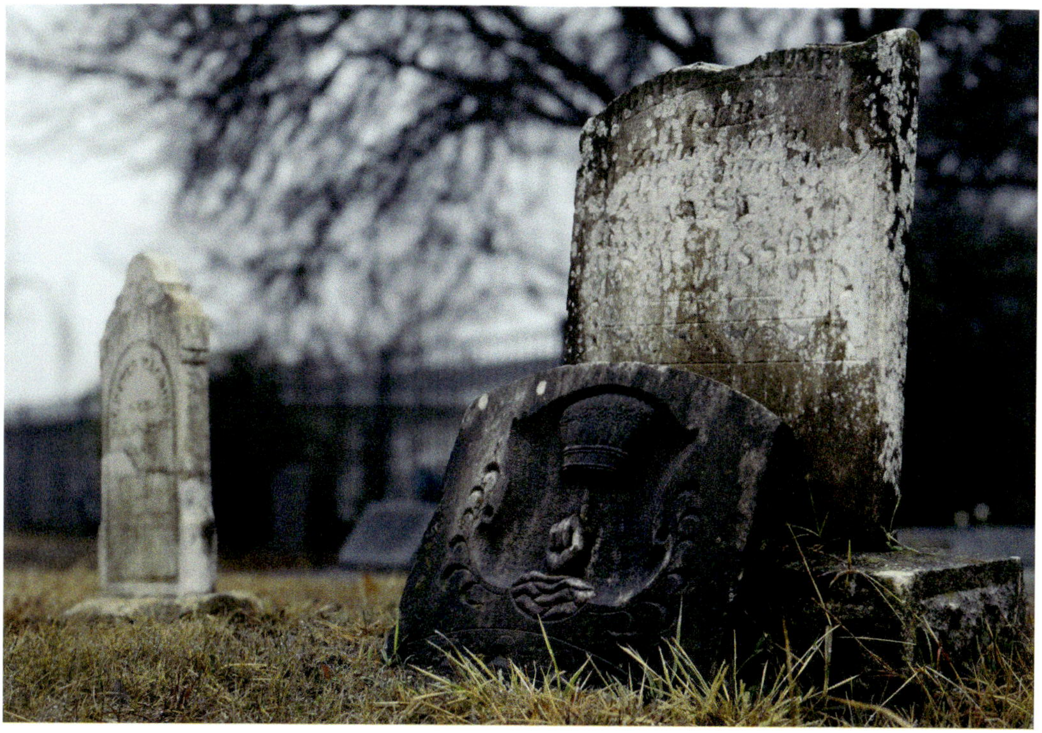

The broken top of the tombstone rests gently upon its base.

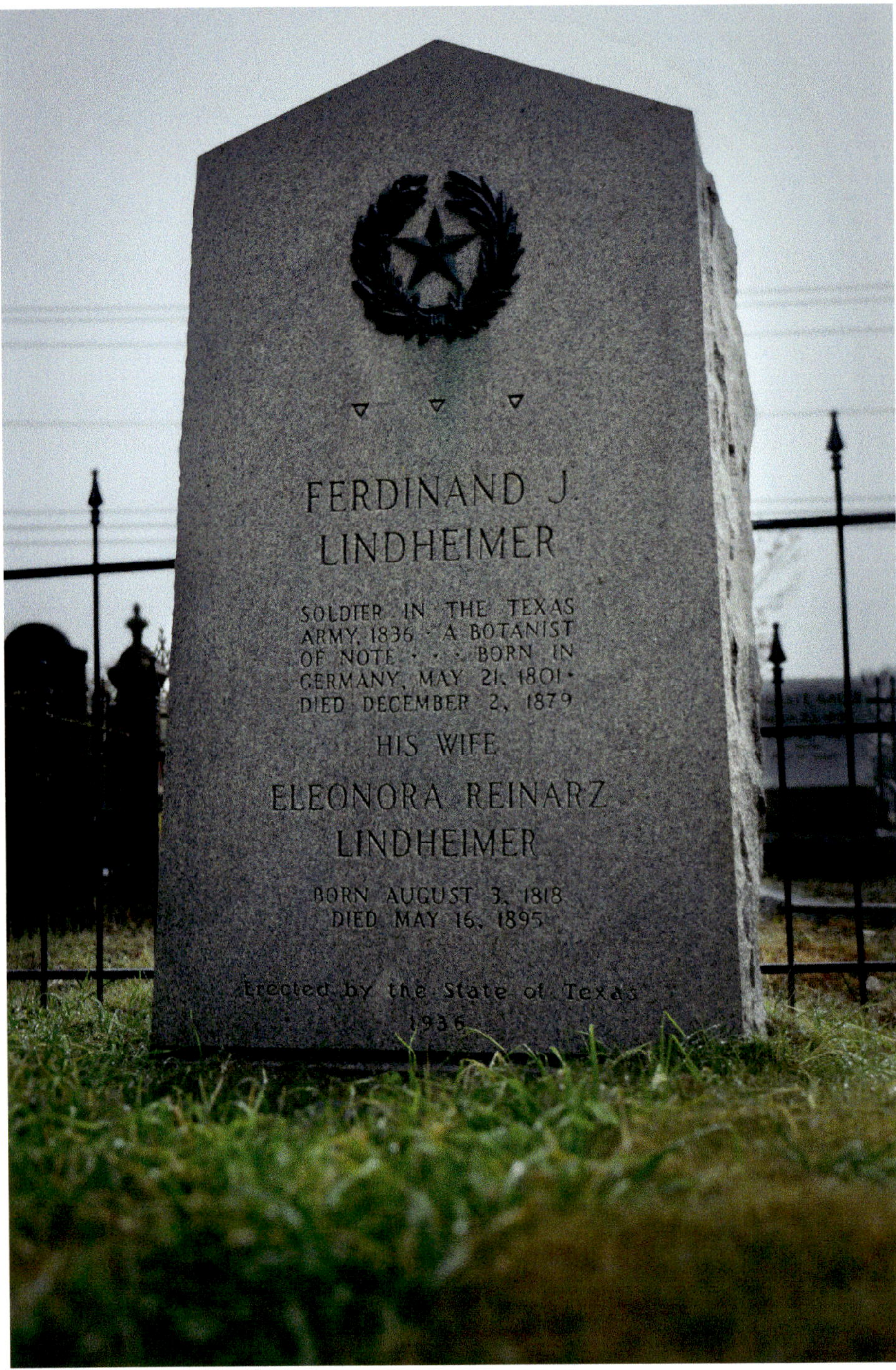

Ferdinand Jakob Lindheimer, known as the "Father of Texas Botany," was a German-Texan botanist and early settler of New Braunfels, Texas. He documented Texas plant life and served as the first editor of the Neu-Braunfelser Zeitung. He is buried in Comal Cemetery.

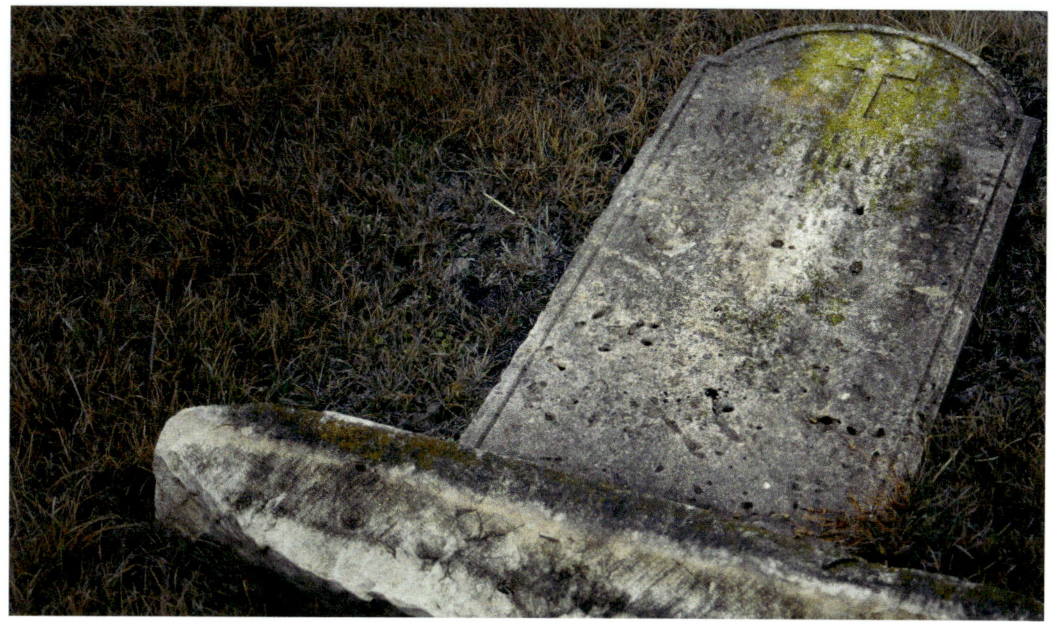

Above: A fallen tombstone, weathered by time and covered in moss, lies partially sunken into the earth.

Right: A beautifully detailed tombstone stands tall, embellished with intricate floral carvings.

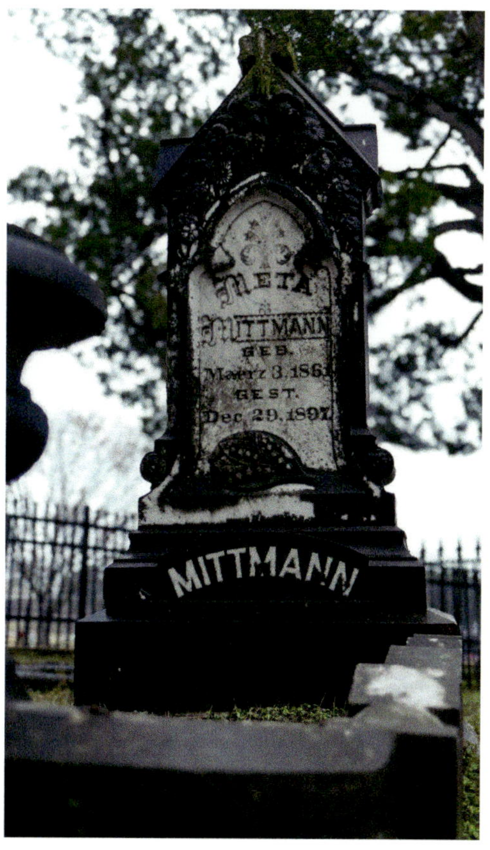

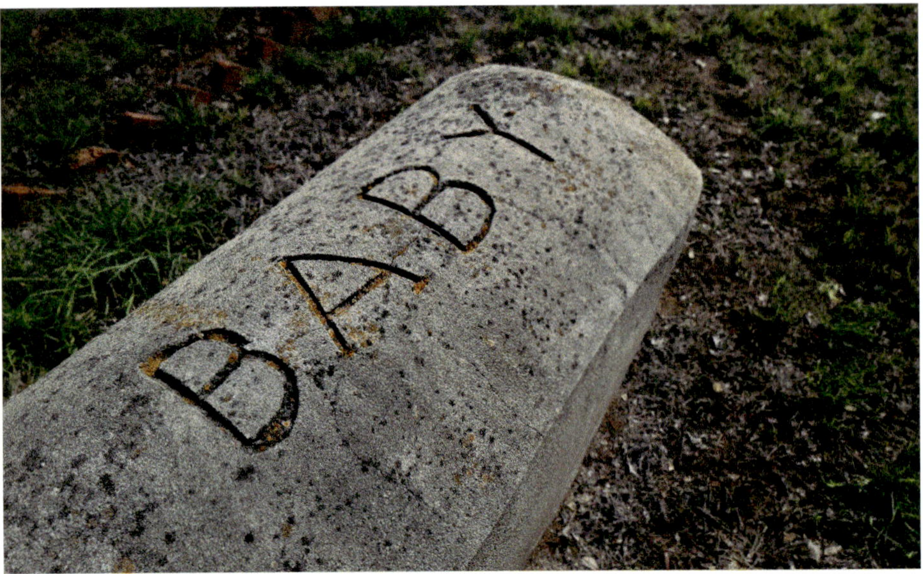

A weathered stone etched with "BABY" stands as a vague yet heartbreaking tribute to a life once loved and lost too soon.

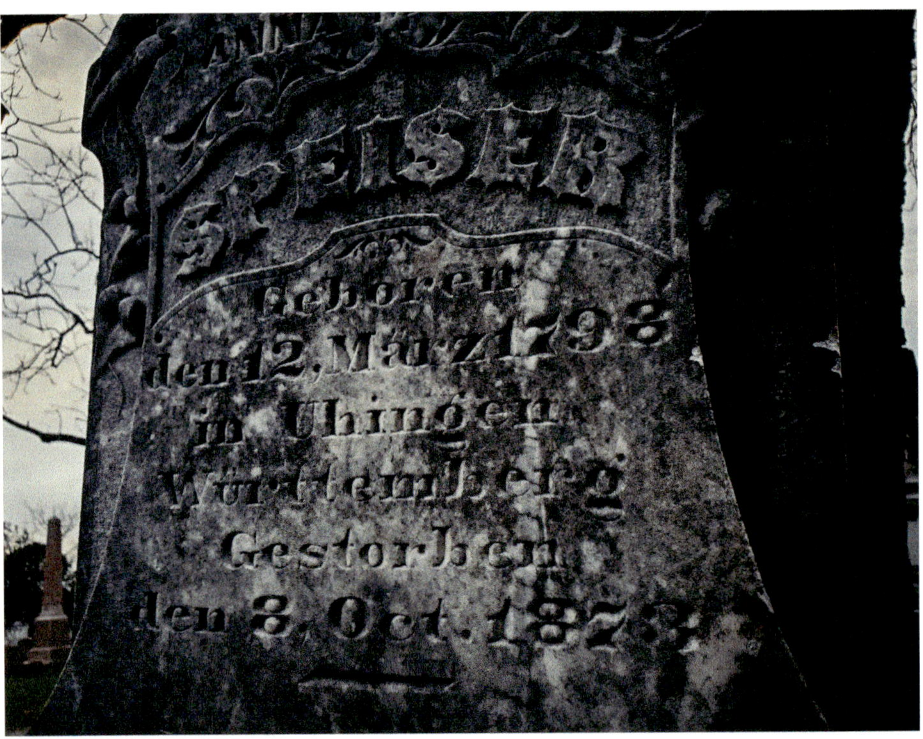

The tombstone of Anna Speiser marks a life that began in Uhingen, Württemberg, and ended in New Braunfels, a lasting link to the past.

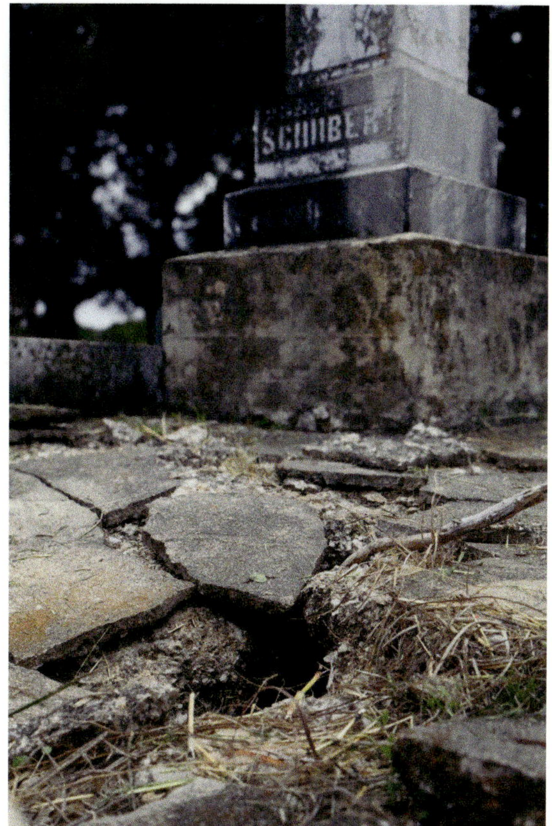

Right: A cracked and sunken gravesite reveals the passage of time, as the foundation crumbles beneath the Schubert tombstone.

Below: This scroll-shaped tombstone, embellished with intricate carvings, has aged over time and is now covered in moss.

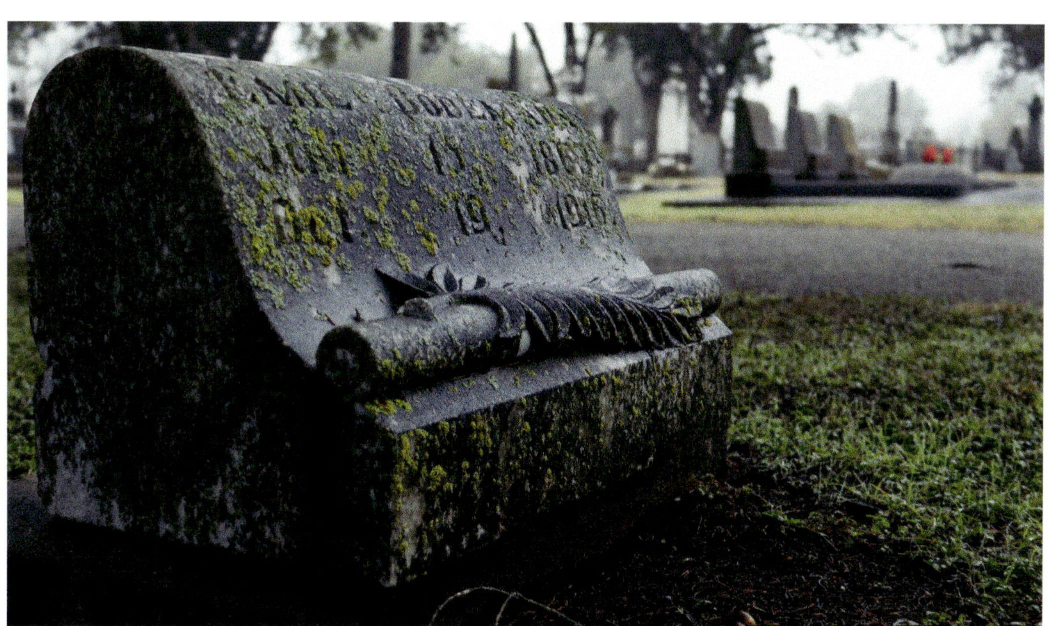

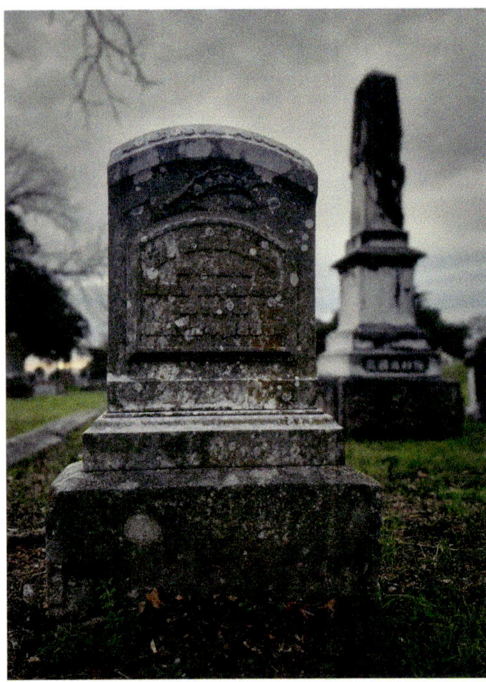

Time has painted this tombstone with patches of lichen, streaks of discoloration, and softened inscriptions, blending stone and nature.

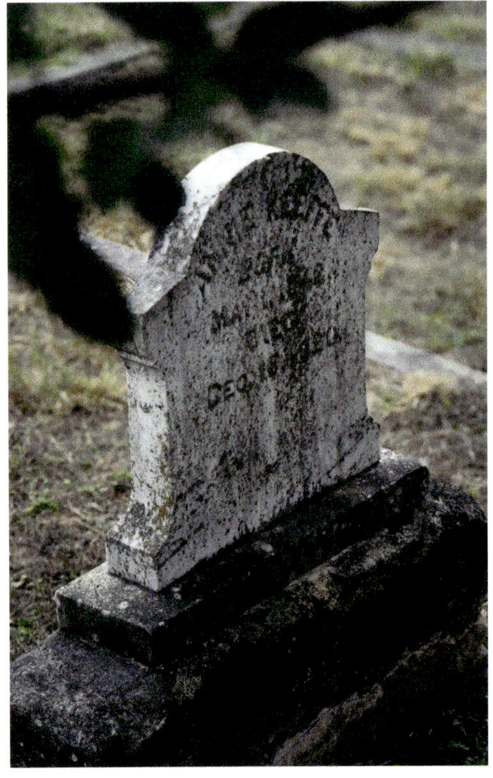

A worn and weathered tombstone, speckled with moss, stands in quiet solitude beneath the overhanging branches.

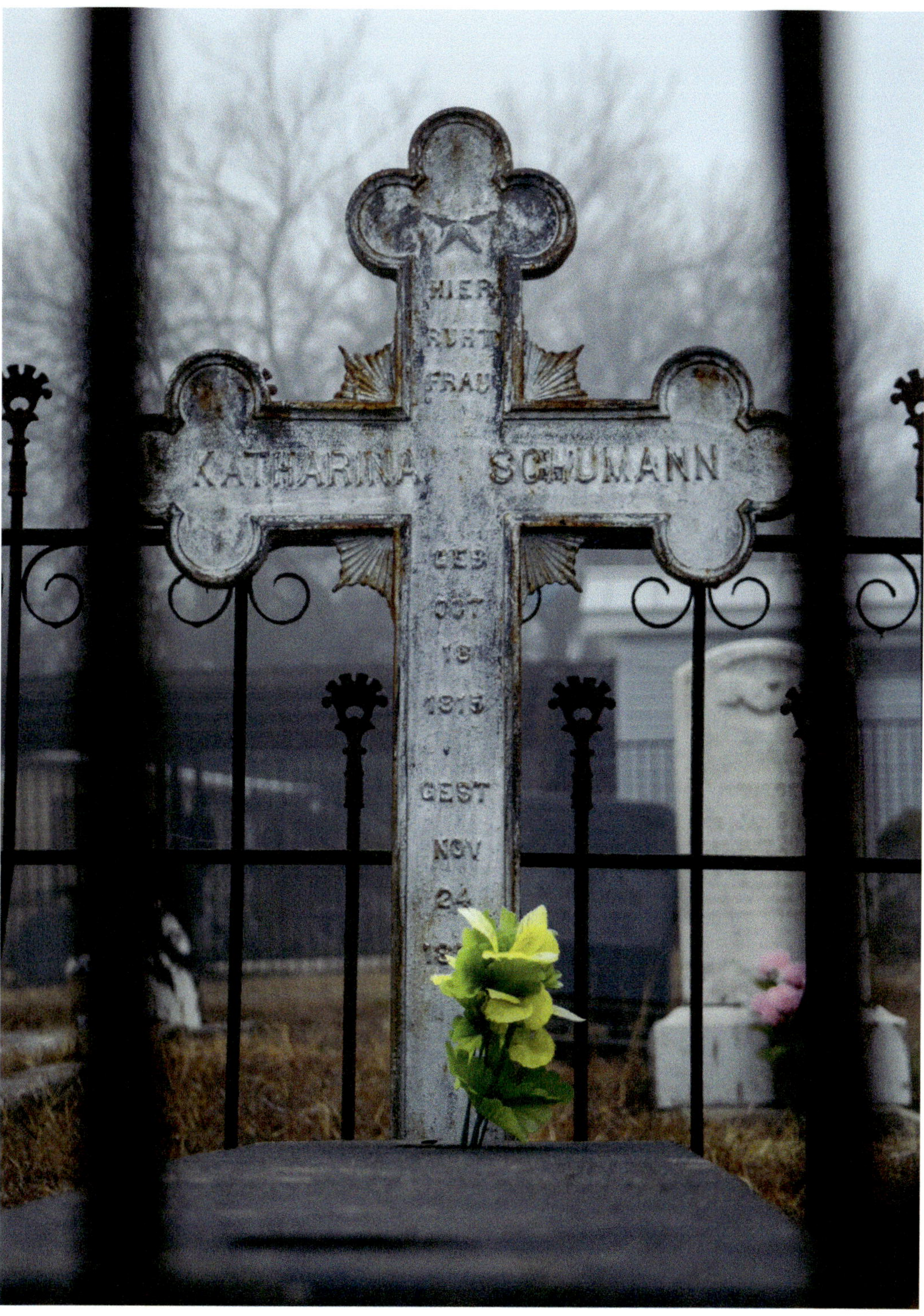

A rusted iron cross marks the grave of Katharina Schumann, standing solemnly behind weathered bars.

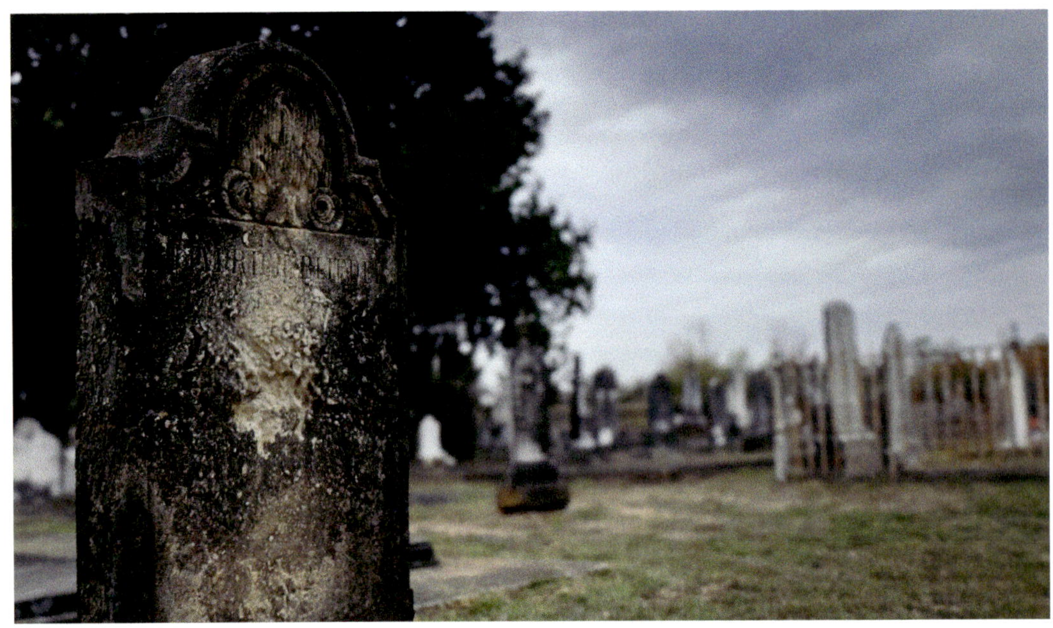

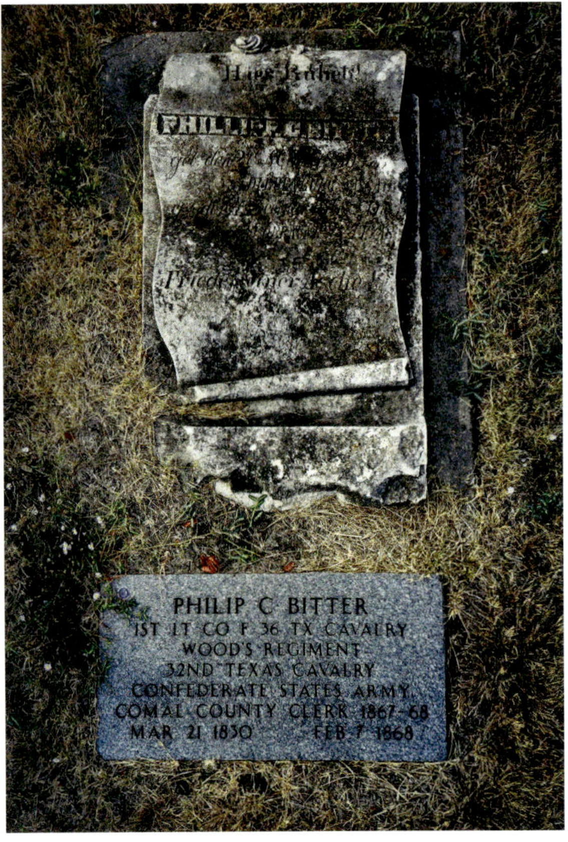

Above: A weathered tombstone, its inscription nearly erased by time, stands alone against a backdrop of aged iron fences and distant graves.

Left: A fractured tombstone tells the passage of time, while a newer marker preserves the legacy of Philip C. Bitter, a Confederate soldier and Comal County Clerk. Two stones, one story, etched in history.

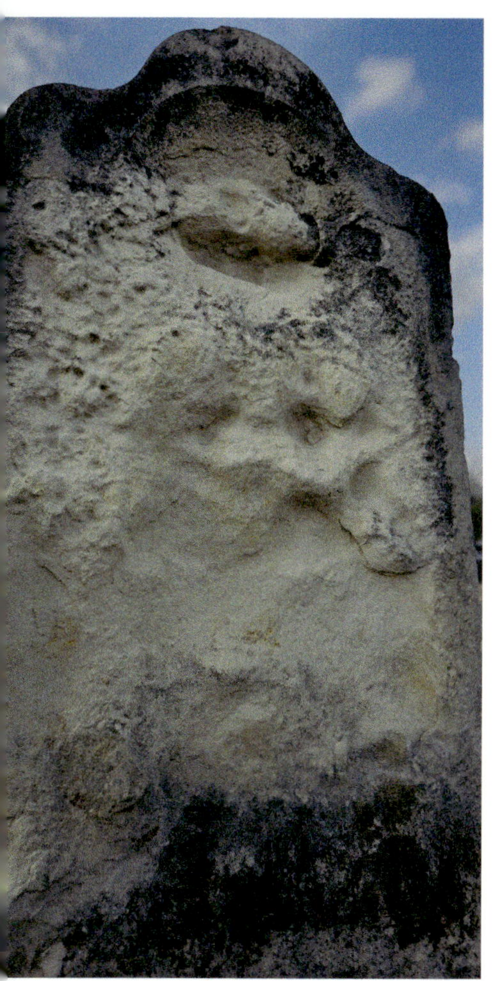

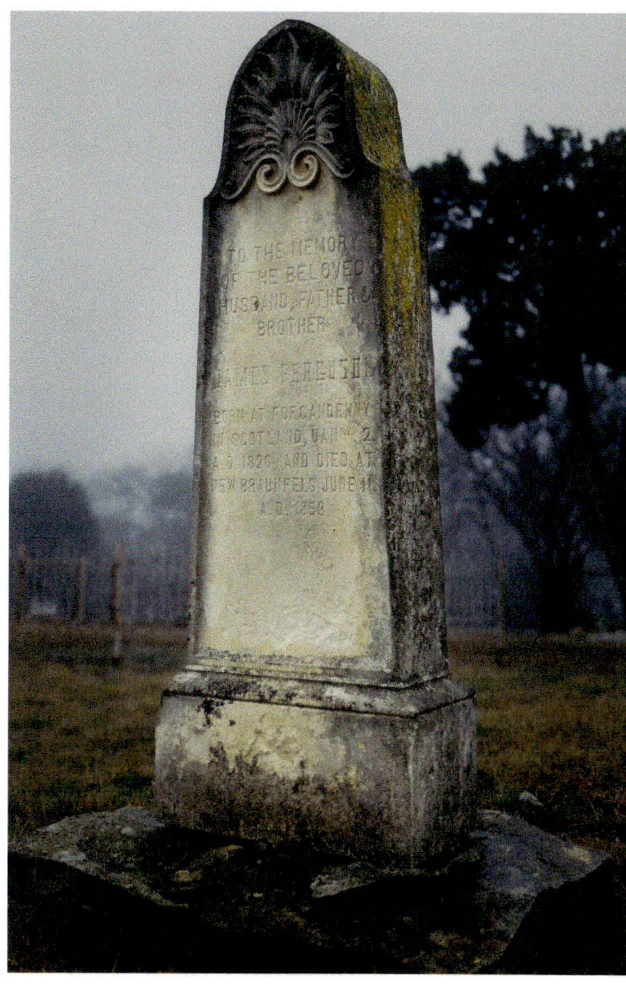

Above left: Eroded by time, this tombstone stands as a silent relic, its inscription lost but its presence enduring.

Above right: This moss-covered monument stands tall on weathered stone, honoring a beloved husband, father, and brother. A journey that began in Scotland and found its final rest in New Braunfels, Texas.

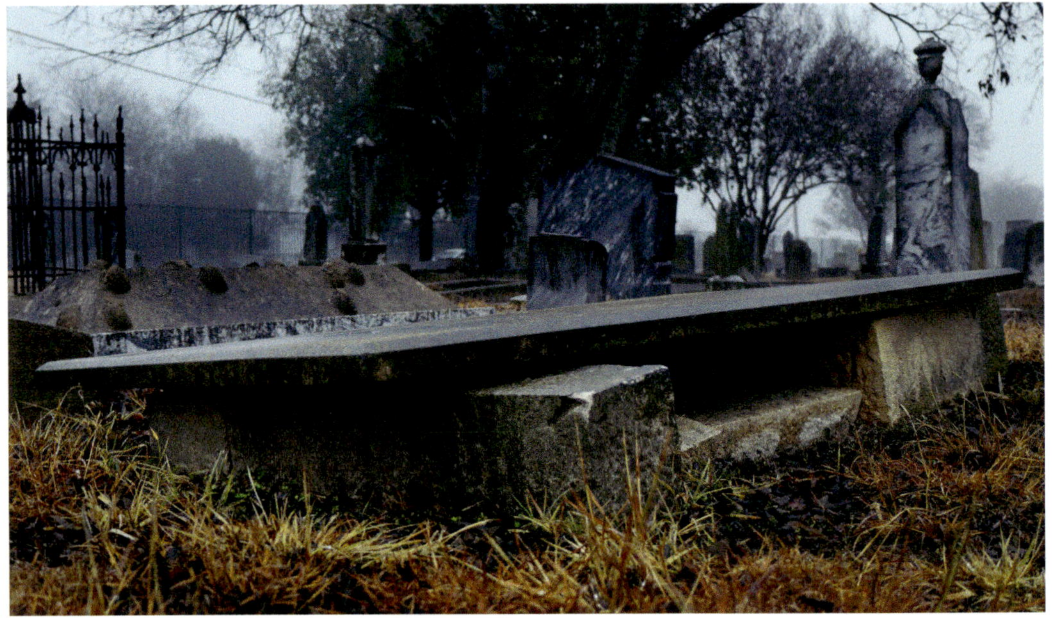

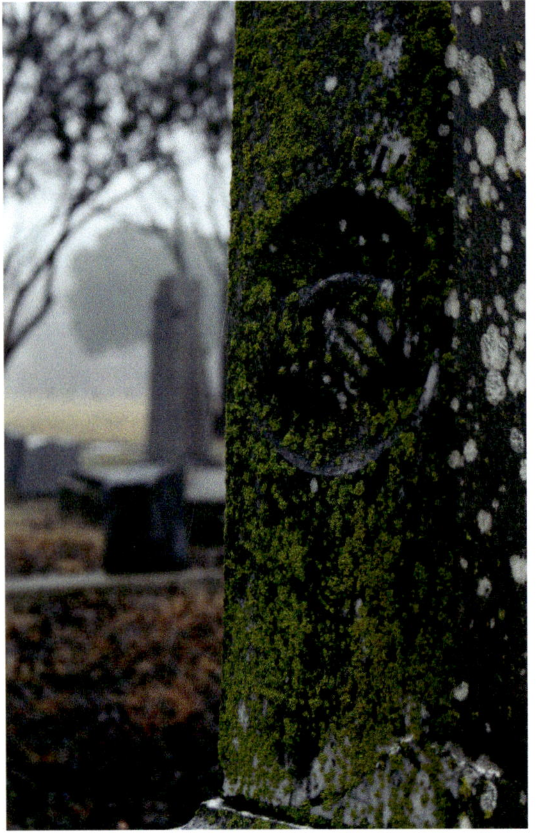

Above: A sunken tomb settles in the misty cemetery, its heavy stone lid displaced by time, echoing the passage of history and the vanishing memories of those laid to rest.

Left: A moss-covered tombstone bears the carved image of a handshake, a symbol of farewell and eternal reunion. Often found on graves, this motif represents a final goodbye between loved ones, a bond unbroken even in death.

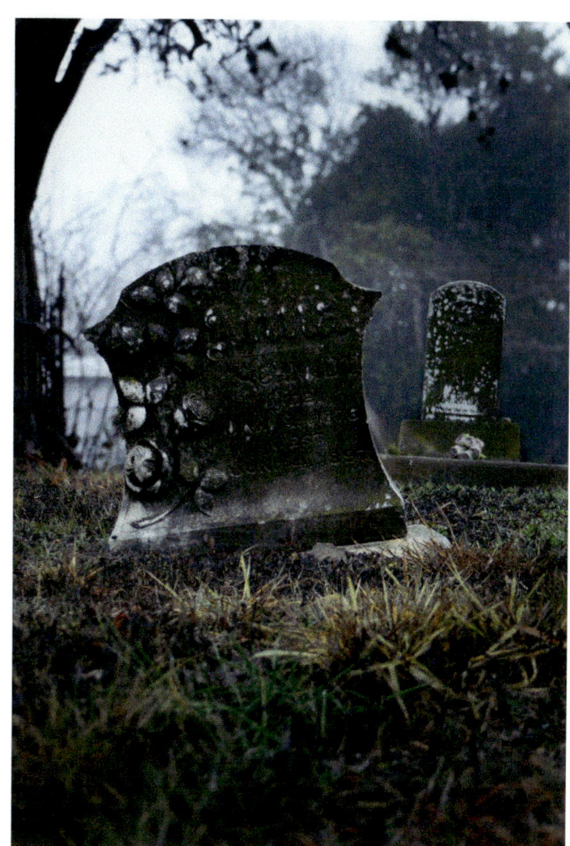

Right: A headstone, embellished with delicate roses and covered in moss, tilts with age.

Below: A broken headstone lies among the earth and fallen leaves.

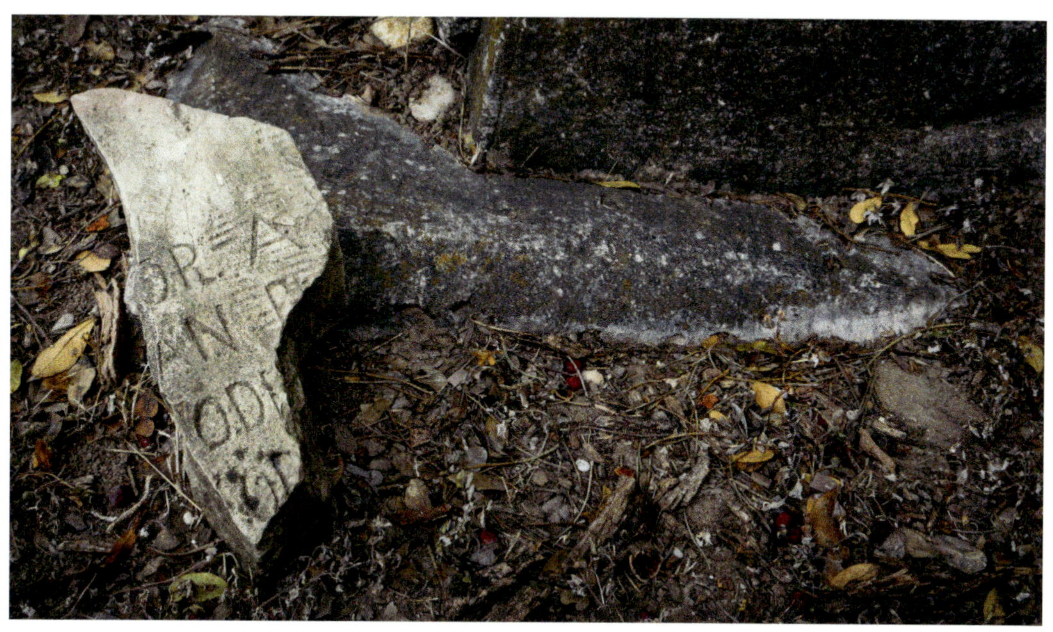

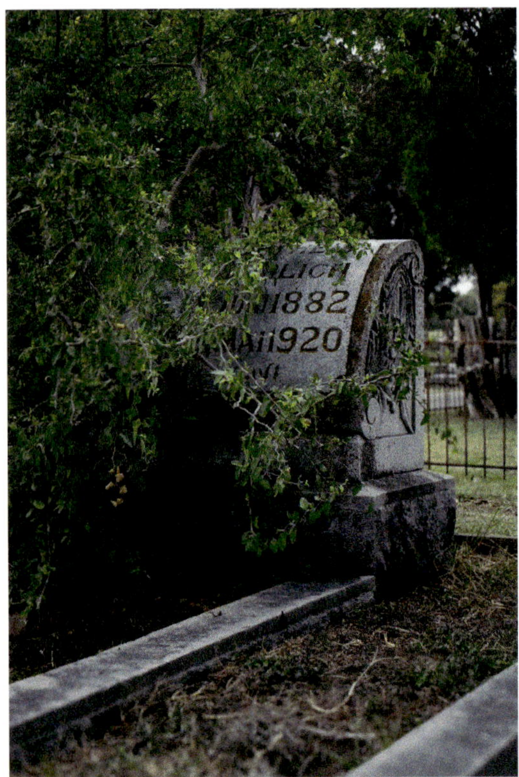

Left: Veiled by overgrown branches, this hidden tombstone quietly fades into the landscape.

Below: Ernst Gruene, founder of Gruene, Texas, built its first mercantile store, cotton gin, and helped establish Gruene Hall. He rests peacefully with his wife, Antoinette, in Comal County Cemetery.

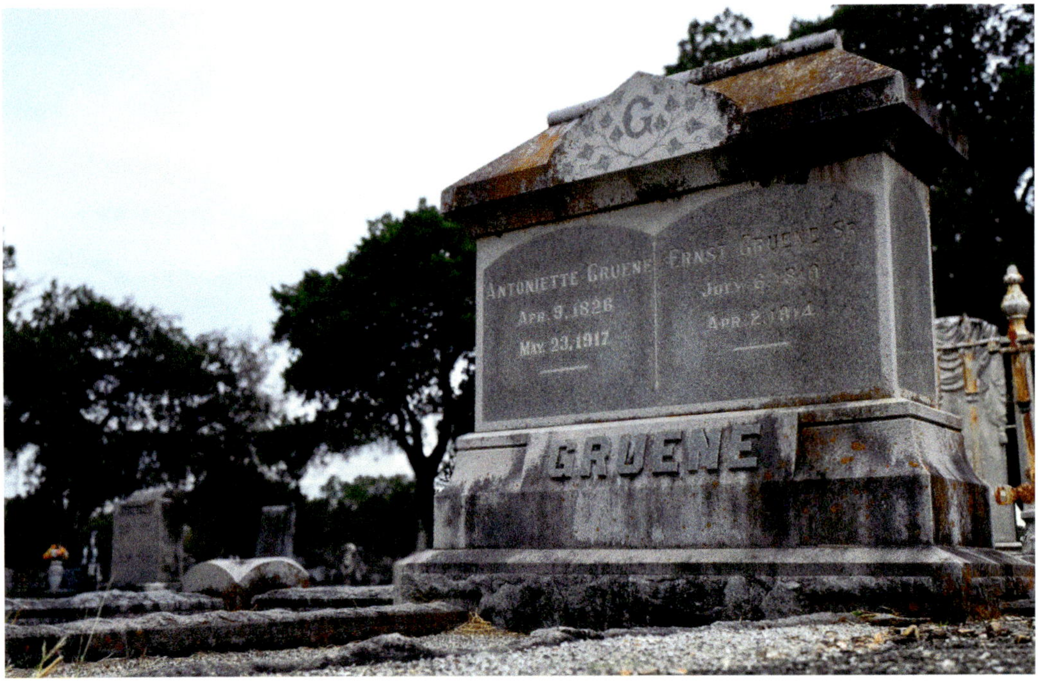

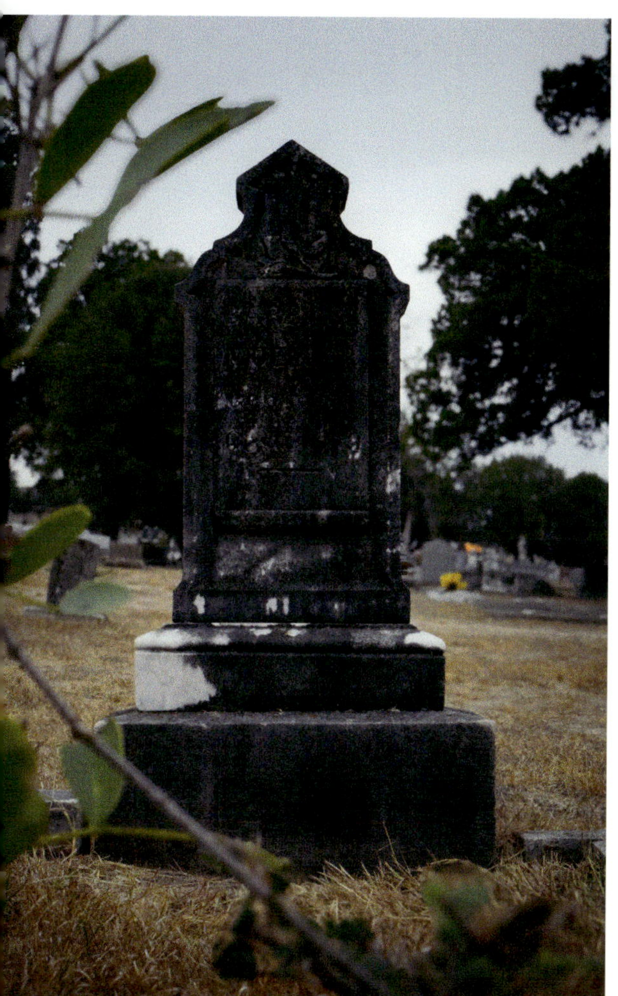

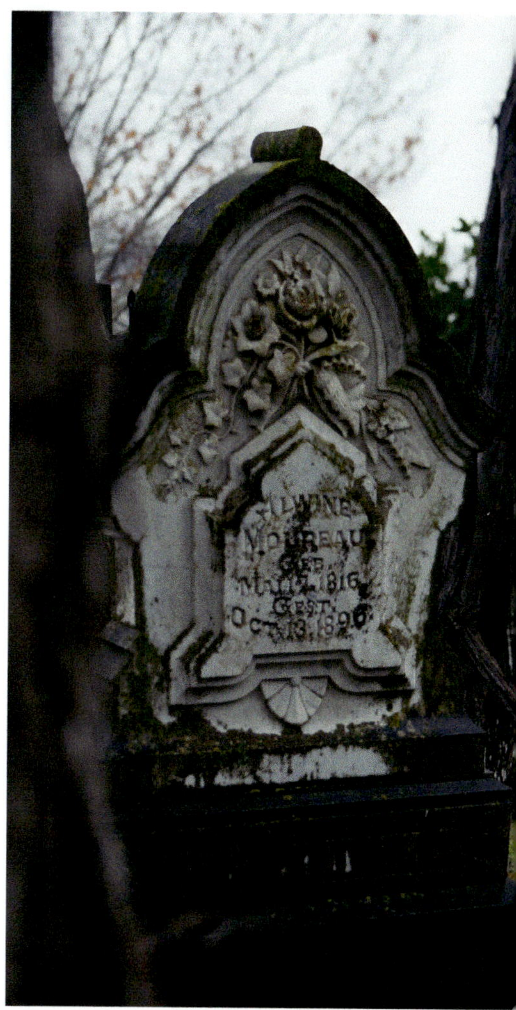

Above left: Framed by creeping leaves, Barbara Moeller's weathered tombstone endures.

Above right: Timeworn and moss-kissed, Alwine Moreau's ornate tombstone stands decorated with delicate carvings.

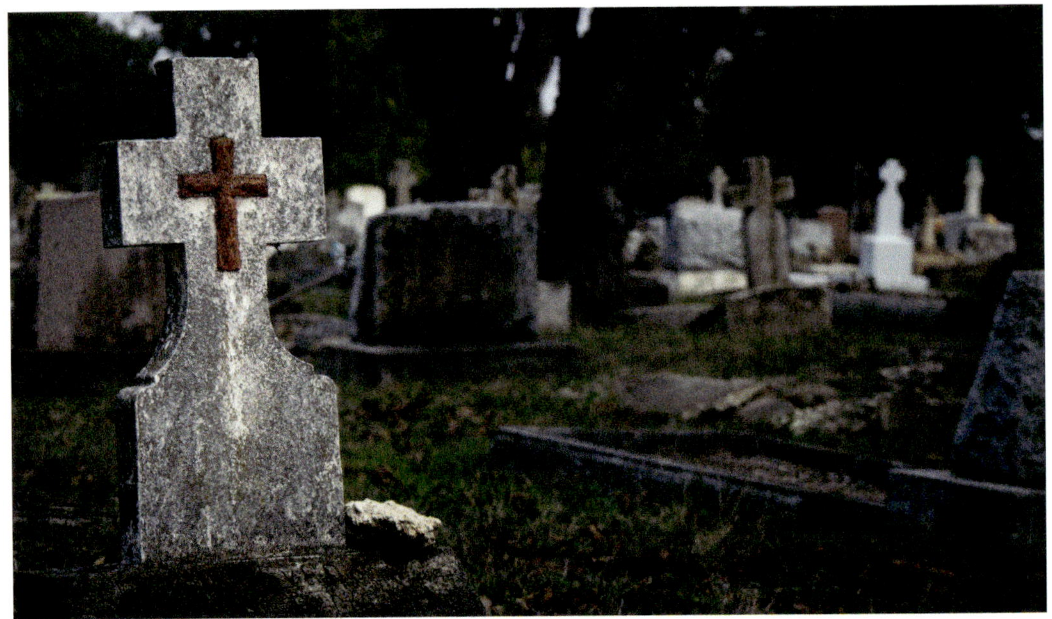

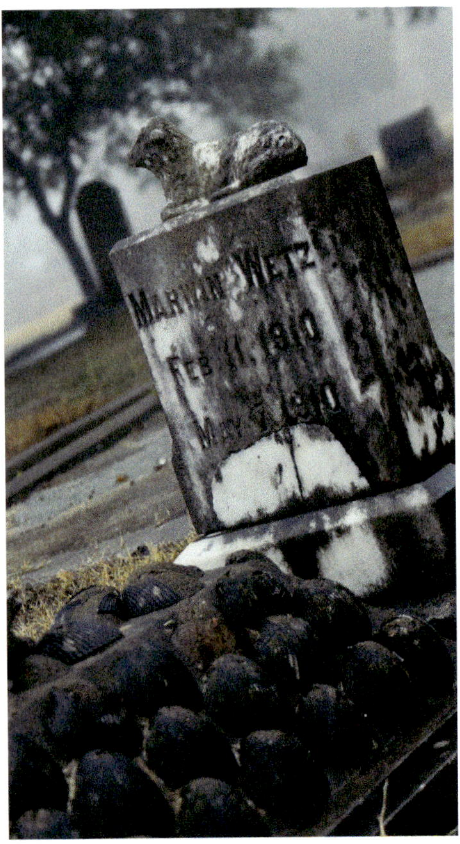

Above: A weathered stone cross, marked by time and rust, stands solemnly among a field of graves, its red cross a stark contrast against the faded stone.

Left: A small, weathered lamb rests atop this infant's grave, a symbol of innocence and peace.

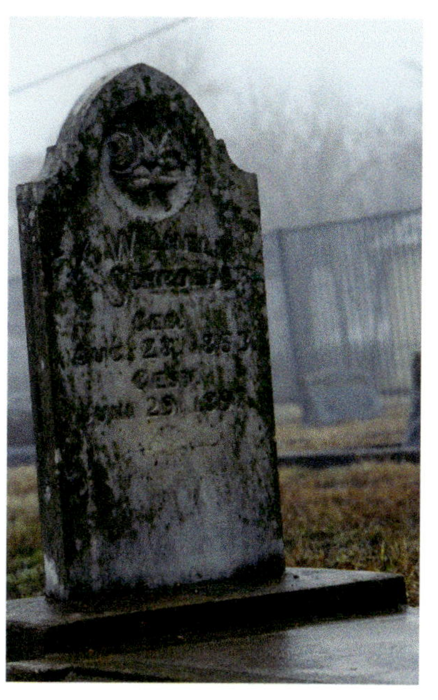

Right: Veiled in moss and timeworn by the elements, F. K. Wilhelm Schroeder's headstone stands in quiet resilience.

Below: Time and nature entwine around the forgotten resting place, where overgrown grass and crumbling stone tell a story of remembrance fading into the past.

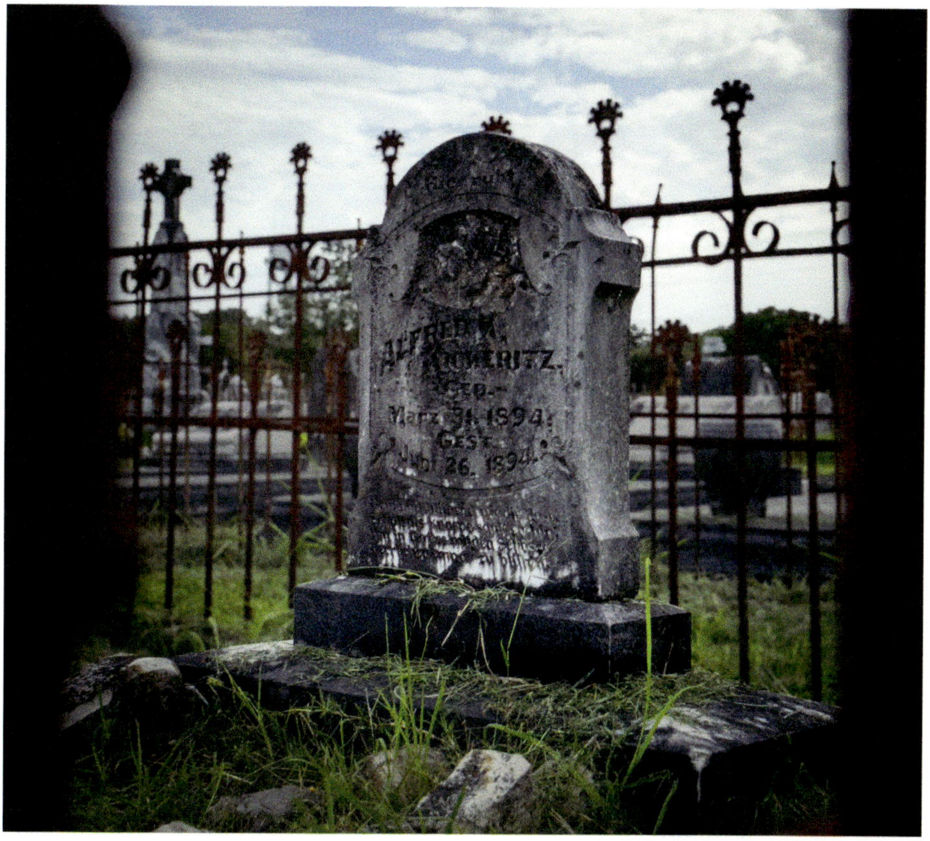

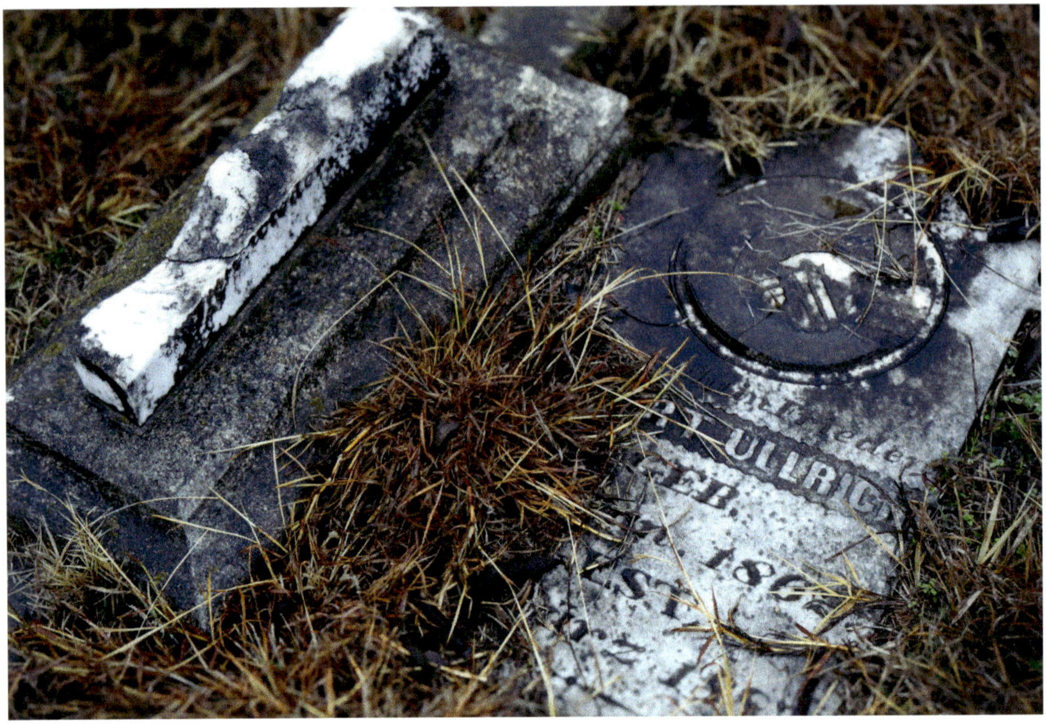

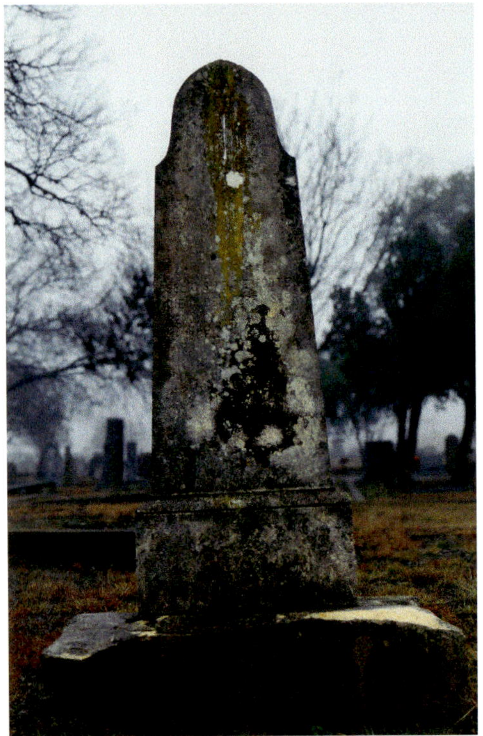

Above: A fallen headstone, partially buried by overgrown grass, bears the symbol of clasped hands, a farewell and a promise of reunion beyond.

Left: This towering headstone bears the inscription, "*Selig sind die Toten, die in dem Herrn sterben von nun an.*" Translated to modern English, it reads: "Blessed are the dead who die in the Lord from now on." (Revelation 14:13).

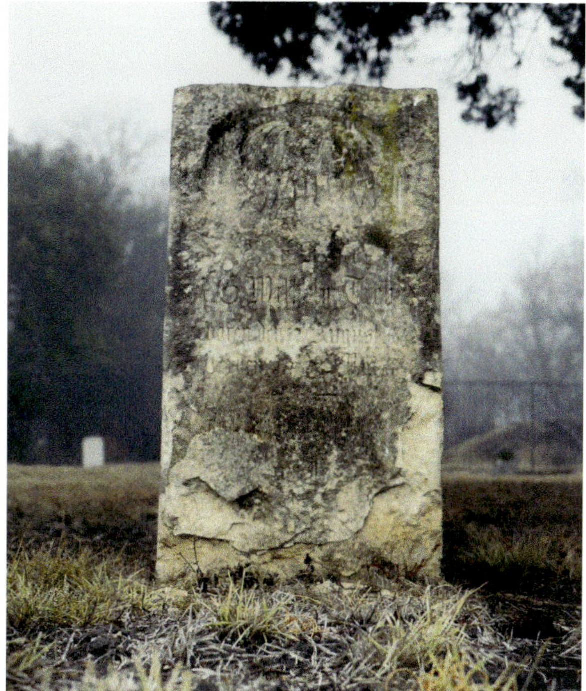

Right: Softened by the elements, this weathered headstone stands as a fading testament to a life once lived. The details may blur, but its presence endures.

Below: A weathered tombstone leans with time, its carved lambs resting beneath a tree in a poignant symbol of peace and innocence.

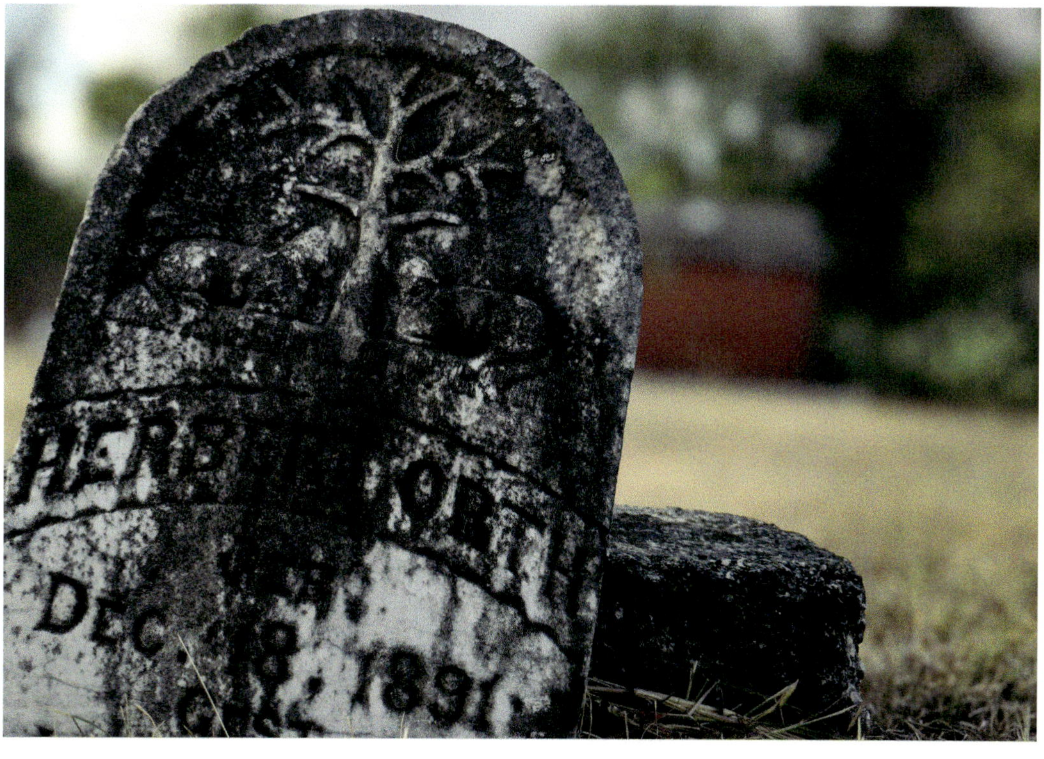

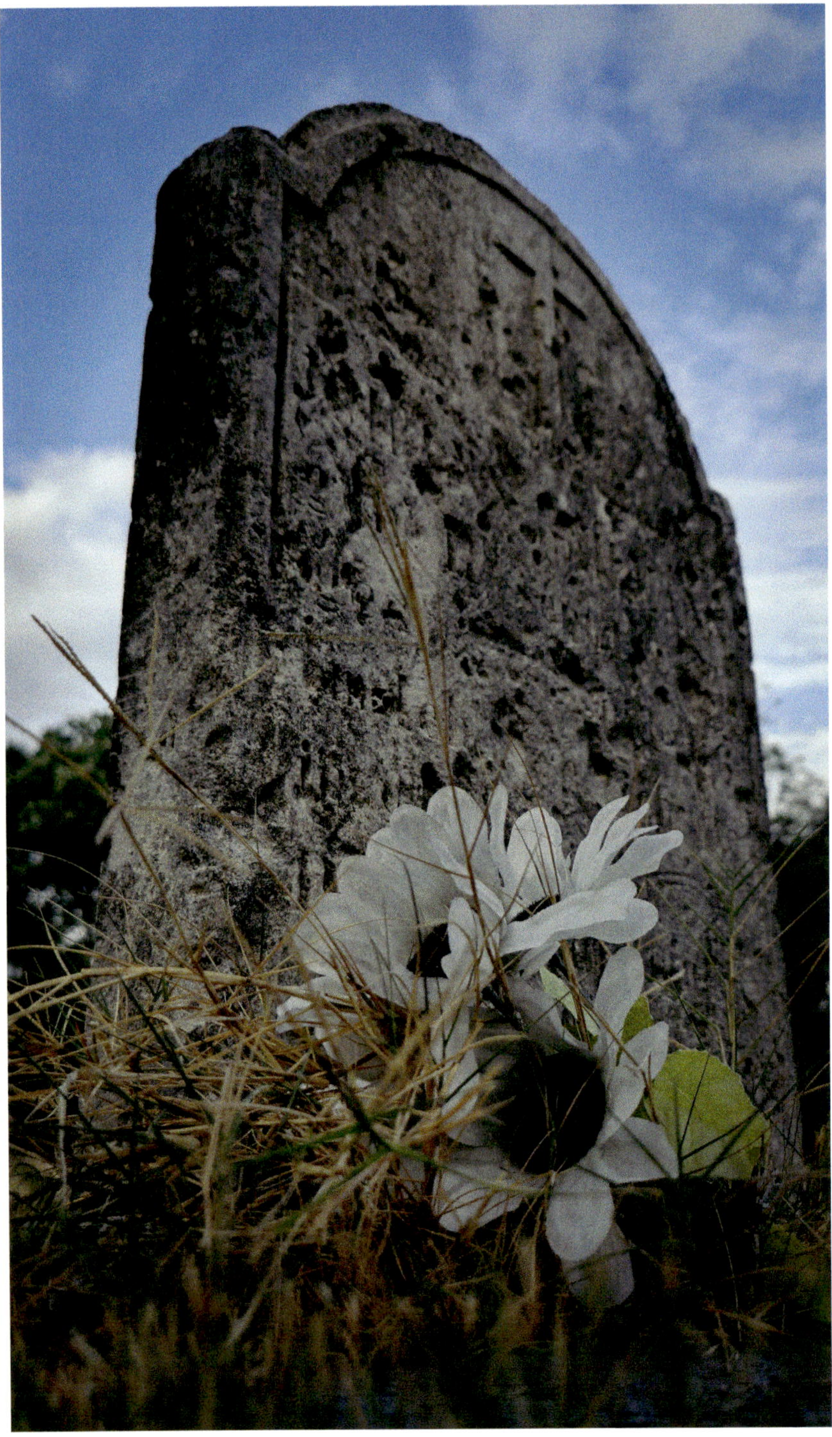

Artificial flowers lay at the base as the headstone. Weathered by time and the elements, it stands tall against the sky.

3
SILENT SENTINELS

The Statues of New Braunfels' Cemeteries

Scattered throughout the cemeteries of New Braunfels stand statues that have watched over the resting for generations. Some are delicate angels with outstretched wings, their faces softened by time, while others are solemn figures, their once-sharp details now worn smooth by decades of wind and rain. Each statue is unique, a reflection of the era and the craftsmanship of those who carved them. Some display intricate, lace-like details, while others stand in quiet simplicity. Weathered by time, many now wear a patina of moss and lichen, adding to their haunting beauty. Cracks and chips mark their long vigil, yet they remain silent guardians of memory and devotion. In this chapter, we explore these remarkable sculptures, capturing their elegance, decay, and the quiet stories they tell.

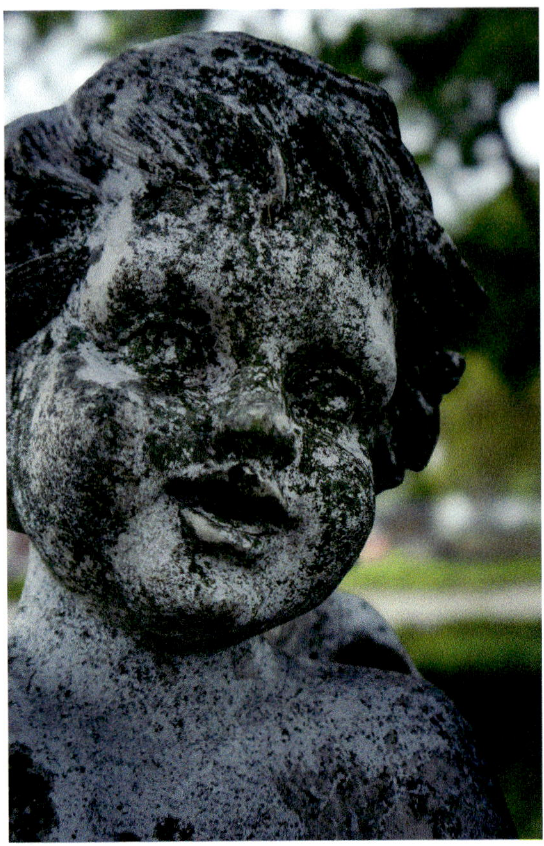

Left: A weathered stone cherub, its face speckled with moss, gazes eternally with a serene yet haunting expression.

Below: A solemn figure, cloaked in moss, stands watch over the graves.

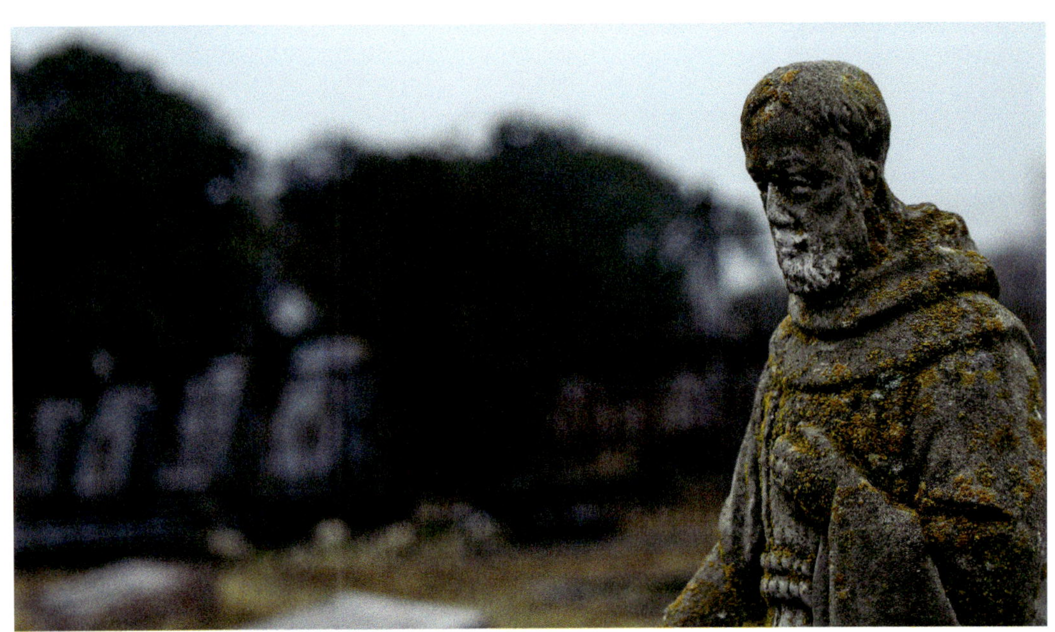

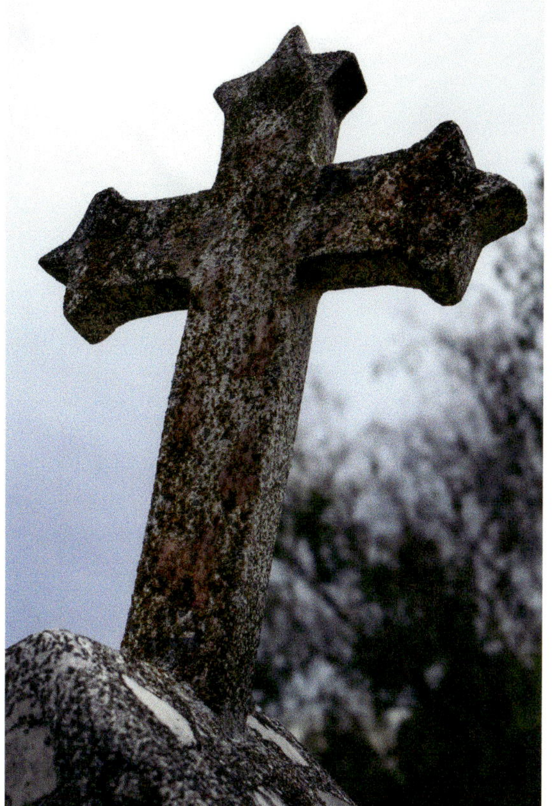

Right: A silent testament of faith and remembrance, this cross stands tall against the sky.

Below: With an outstretched arm, this weathered stone statue of Christ stands in quiet reverence, its gaze unwavering. Time and the elements have left their mark, yet its message of grace and guidance endures.

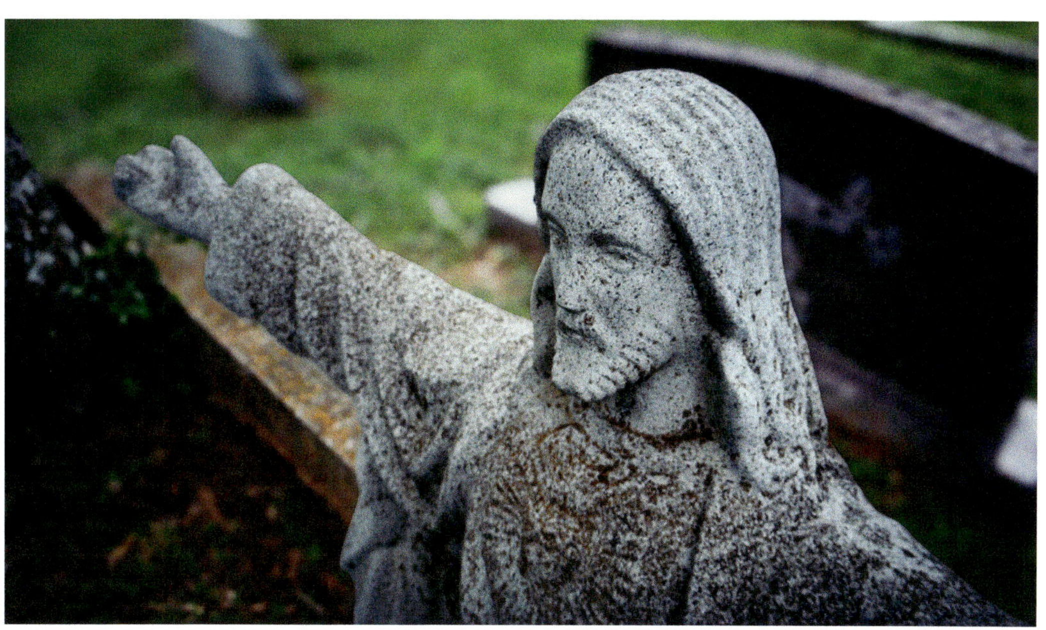

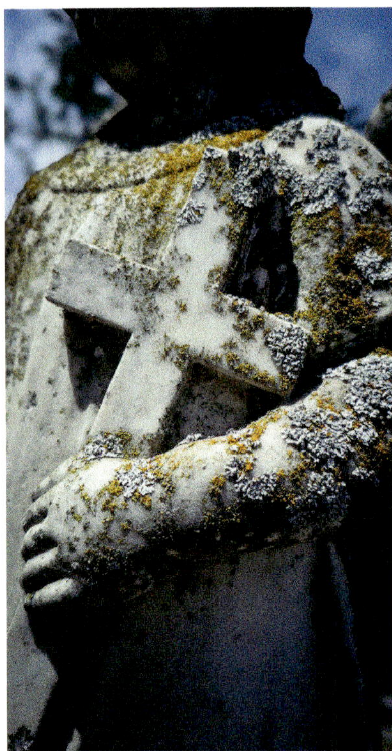

Left: Covered in moss and lichen, this aged statue clutches a cross.

Below: This solemn statue of the Pietà captures a moment of grief and devotion. Moss and lichen creep along the stone, as nature slowly embraces the sorrowful embrace of mother and son.

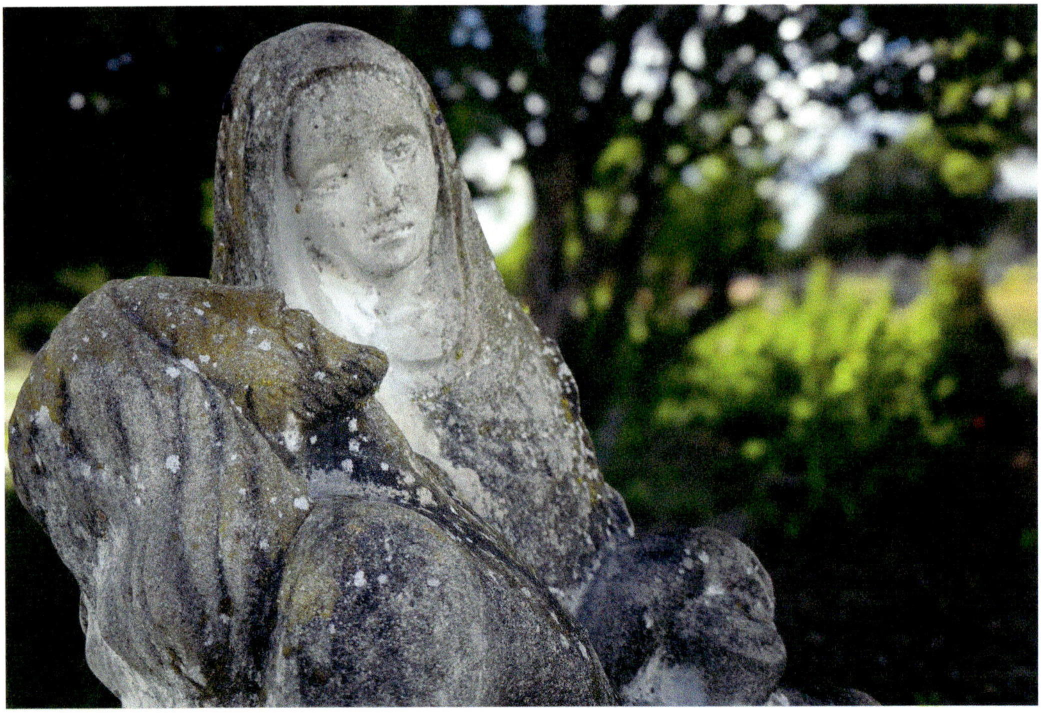

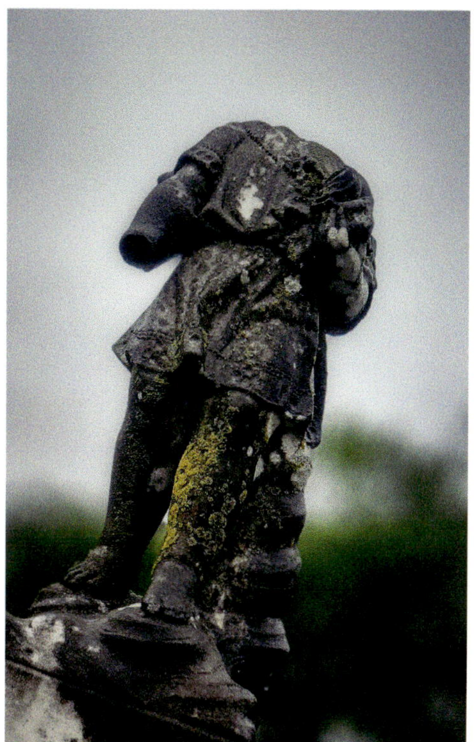

Even in ruin, this statue stands, weathered and broken.

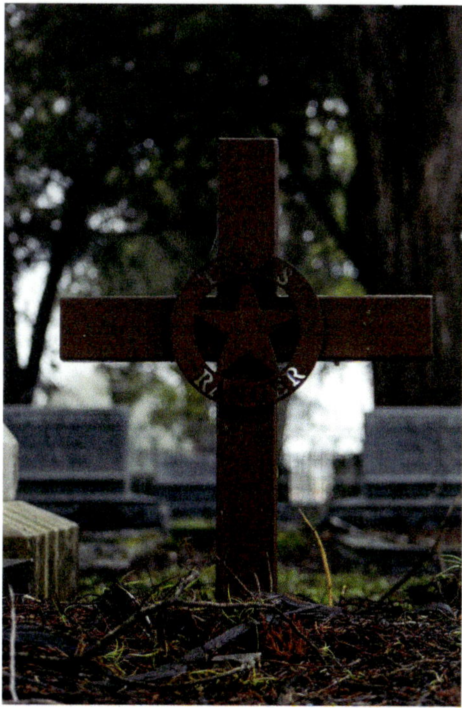

A rusted cross bearing the Texas Rangers emblem stands in remembrance, honoring the legacy of one of the nation's oldest and most storied law enforcement agencies.

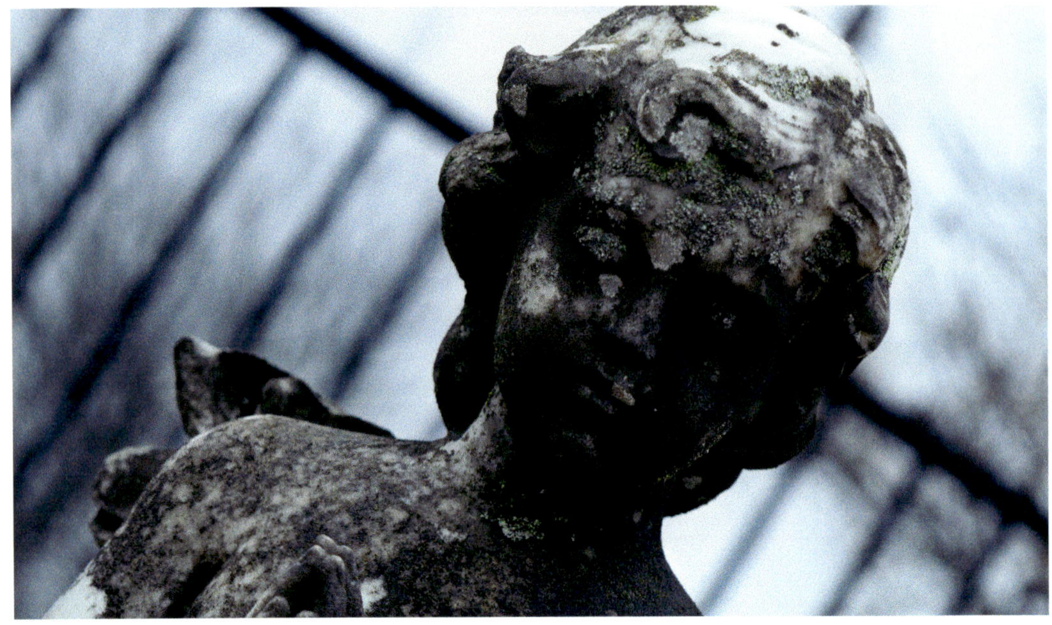

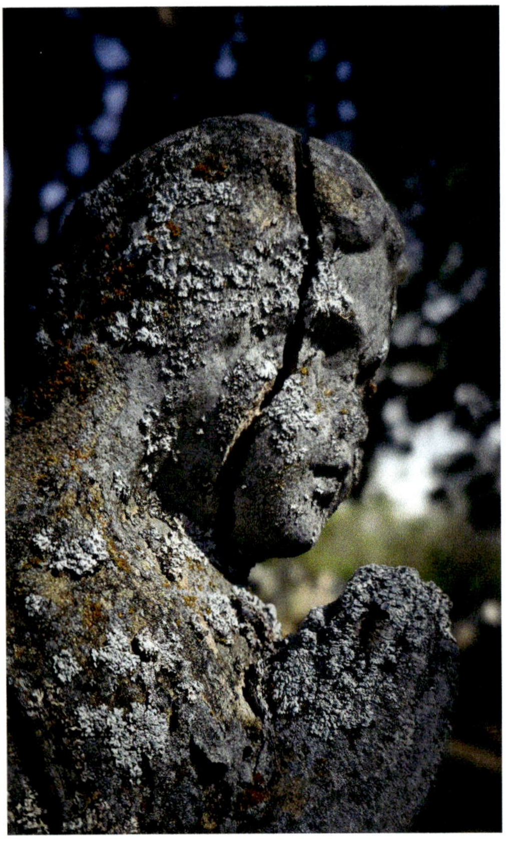

Above: Once a pristine marble cherub, time and sorrow have left their mark upon its delicate form.

Left: A fractured stone figure, its surface rough and worn, stands frozen in time, hands clasped in a silent prayer.

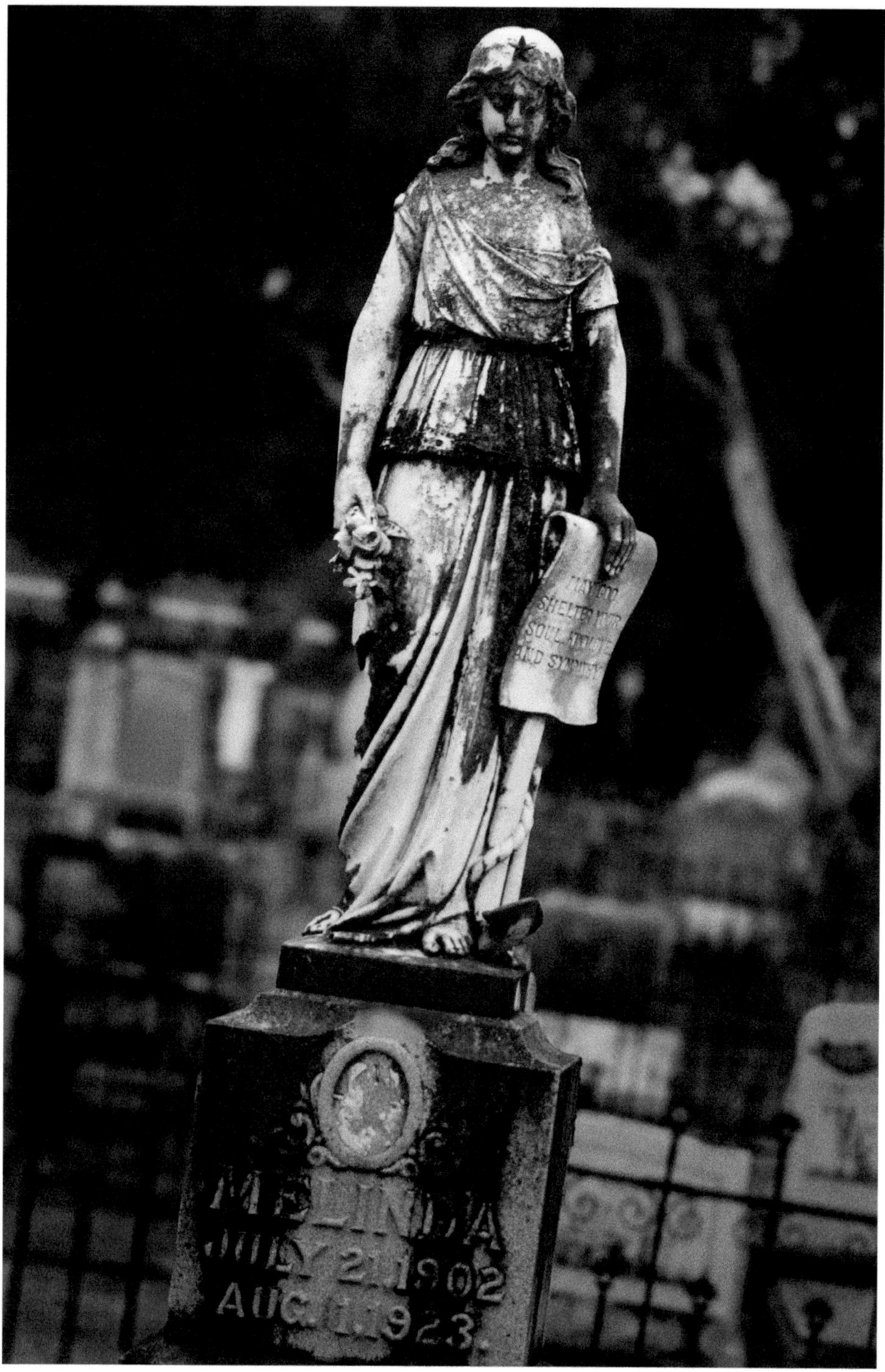

Clutching a scroll and fading flowers, this solemn figure watches over Melinda's resting place, a silent guardian of a life gone too soon.

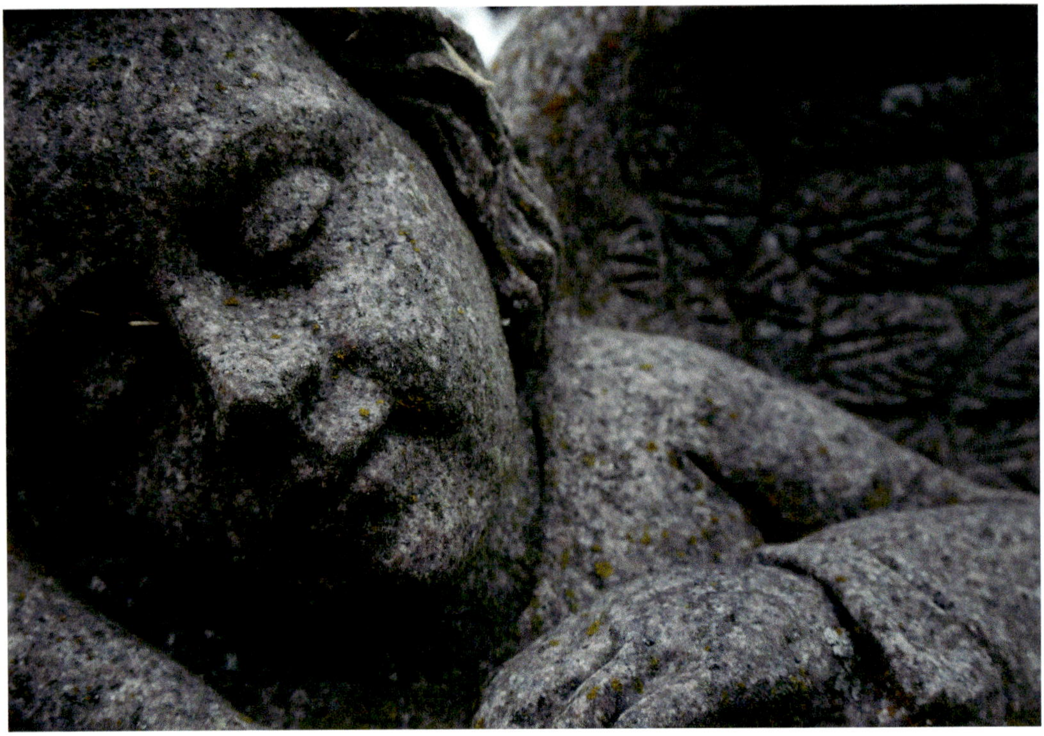

Wings of this cherub, once symbols of flight, now bear the weight of time, frozen in silent vigil over the departed.

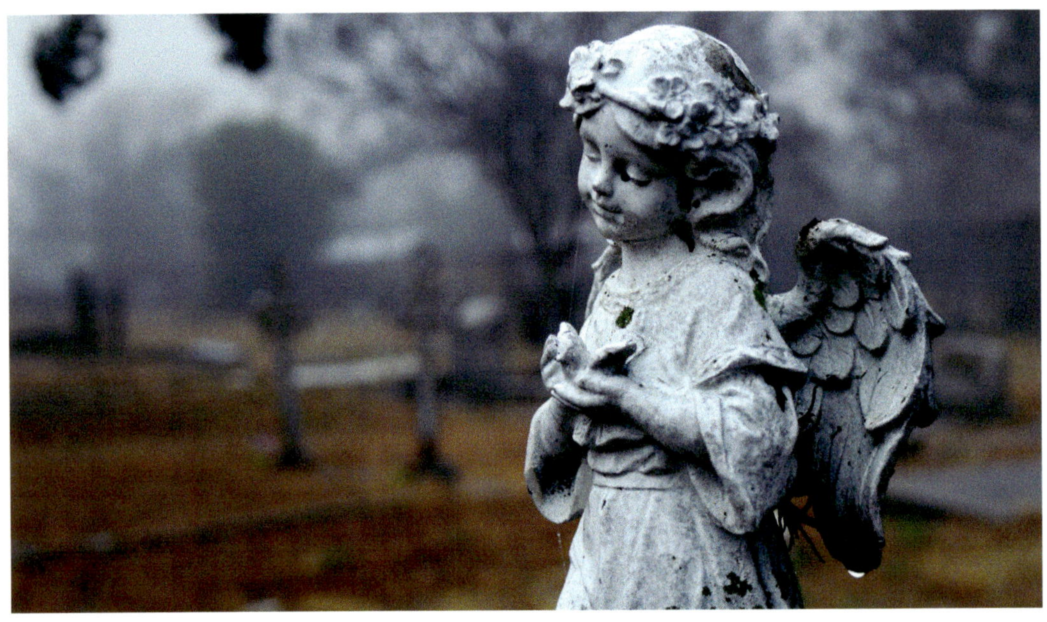

A delicate stone angel stands amidst the mist, its small hands cradling a bird in eternal stillness.

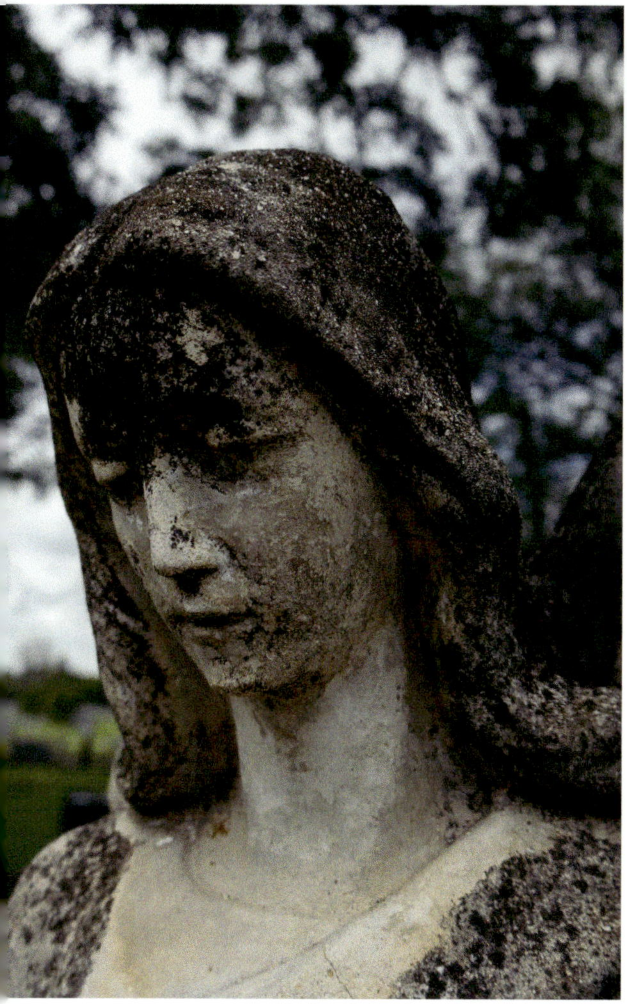

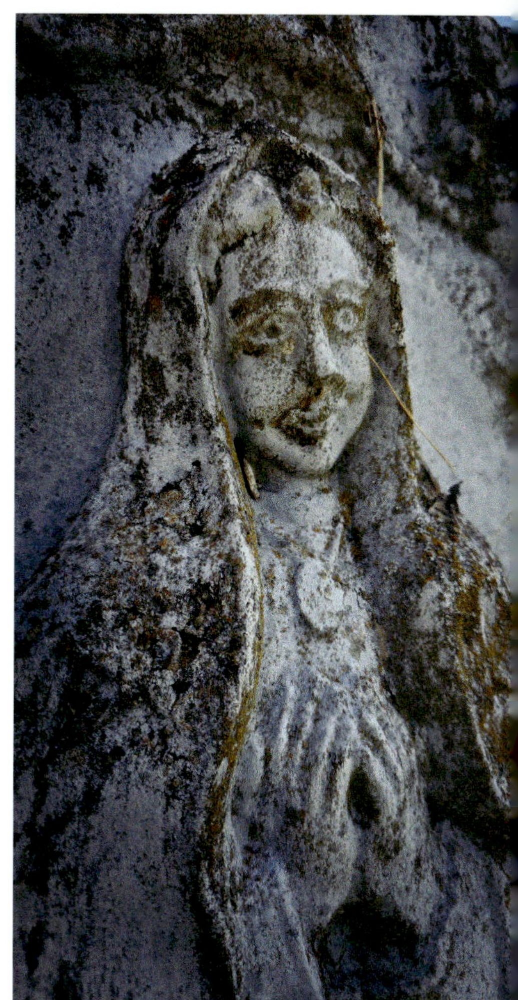

Above left: An angel stands in quiet contemplation, her downcast eyes heavy with an unspoken sorrow.

Above right: Time etches its mark on this weathered figure of the Virgin Mary.

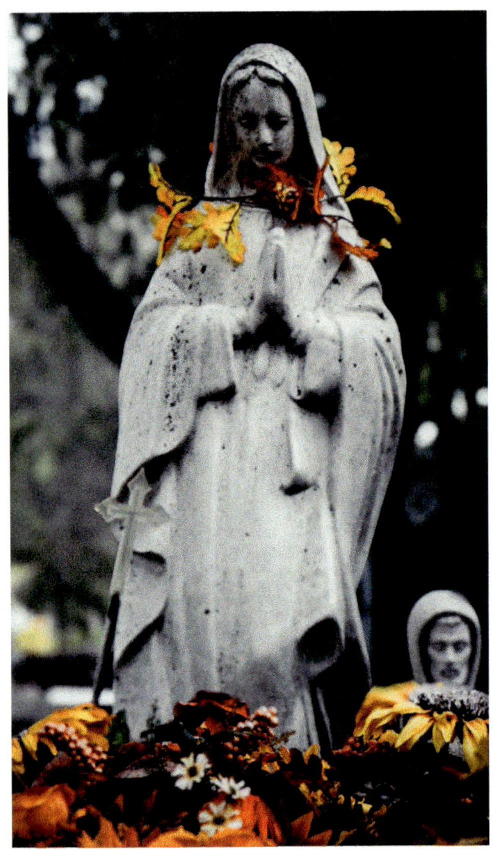

Left: A solemn statue draped in autumn's embrace, standing in silent prayer amid a bed of vibrant flowers, a contrast of fading stone and fleeting beauty.

Below: A cherub, hands clasped in prayer, face veiled in lichen, stands against the misty backdrop.

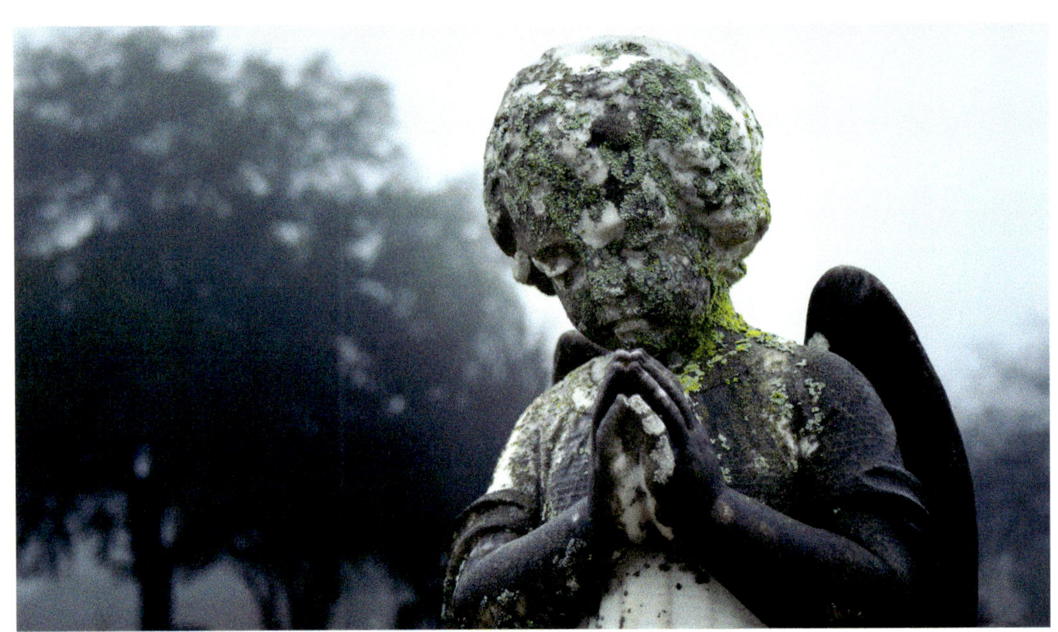

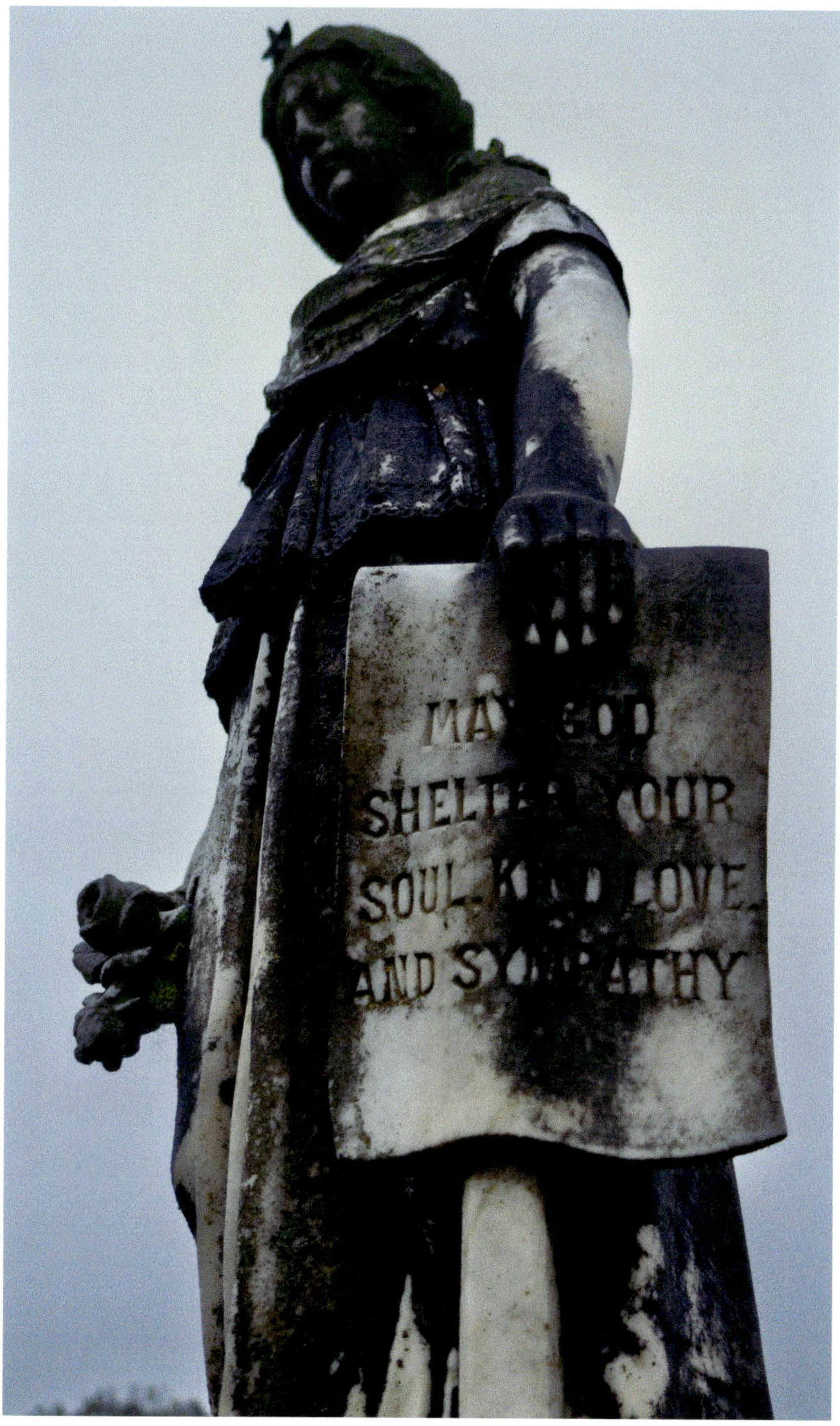

"May God shelter your soul, kind love, and sympathy," a whisper of solace etched in stone.

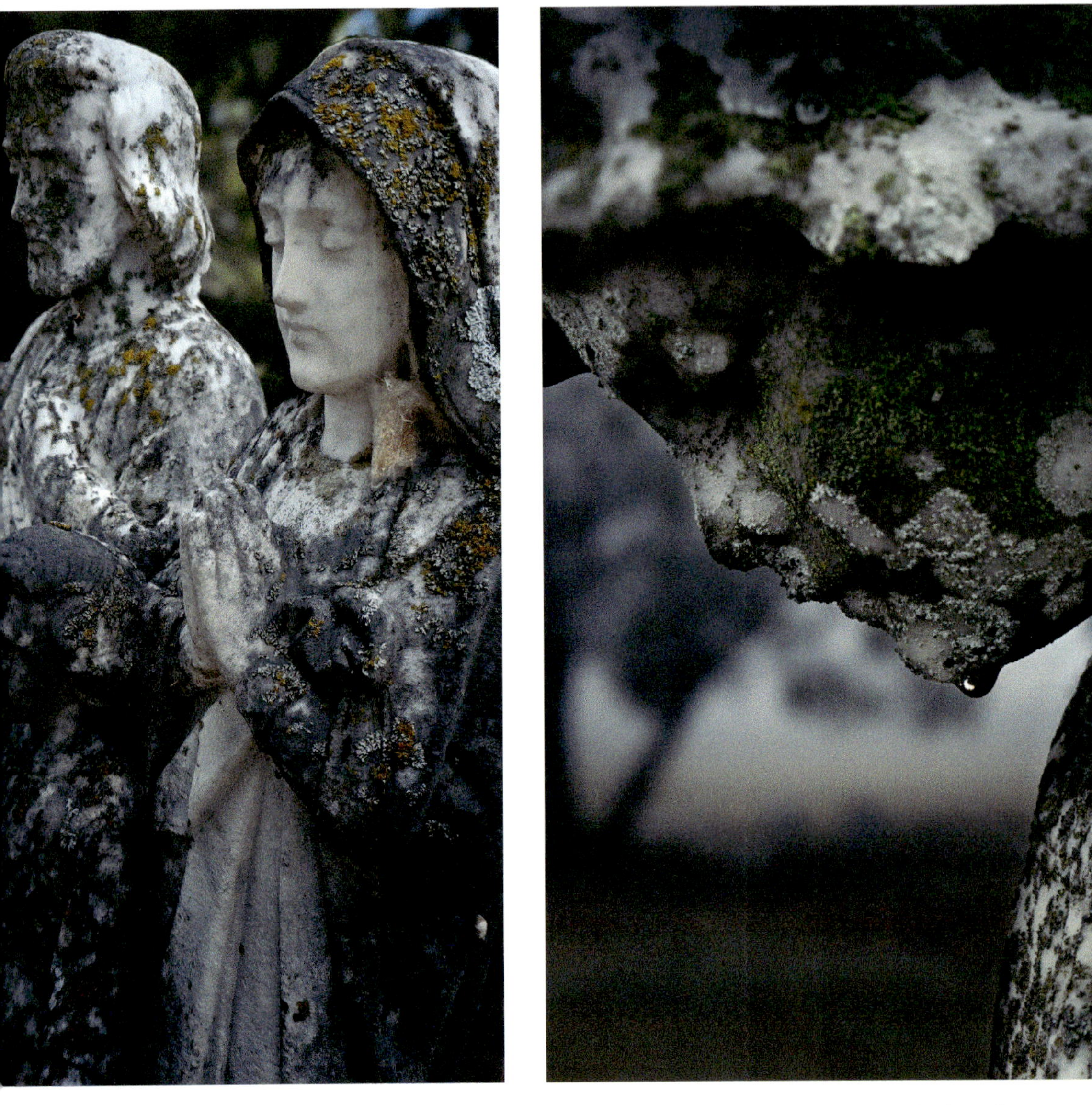

Above left: Hands clasped in eternal prayer, these two stand as a quiet testament to faith and devotion.

Above right: A solitary drop clings to the weathered stone, suspended in time like a tear of the heavens, moss and lichen embracing the angel's face.

4
Time Carved in Stone

The Intricate Details of Cemetery Art

Every corner of New Braunfels' historic cemeteries holds a testament to craftsmanship, devotion, and the passage of time. Many of the headstones and statues are adorned with intricate carvings, including delicate floral engravings, carefully chiseled names, and lifelike stone figures that once stood crisp and defined. Time has softened their edges, while nature has slowly reclaimed them. Moss and lichen creep along the surfaces, filling in the once-sharp details, blurring the inscriptions, and adding an eerie beauty to the already solemn landscape.

Beyond the stones themselves, artistry can be found in the ironwork that surrounds many of the graves. Elaborate wrought-iron fences, rusted but still standing, frame family plots with swirling patterns and ornate flourishes, each a unique creation of a blacksmith's skilled hands. Some graves are topped with seashells, a quiet tradition that leaves behind its own mystery, while others are marked by tree-stump headstones, their carved bark so textured and lifelike that it seems as if it could still be rough to the touch. These details, both small and large, fading yet enduring, are more than just decoration. They are pieces of history, crafted with care and intention, each a final tribute from those who came before. In this chapter, we take a closer look at the artistry left behind, the weathering of time, and the haunting beauty hidden in the details.

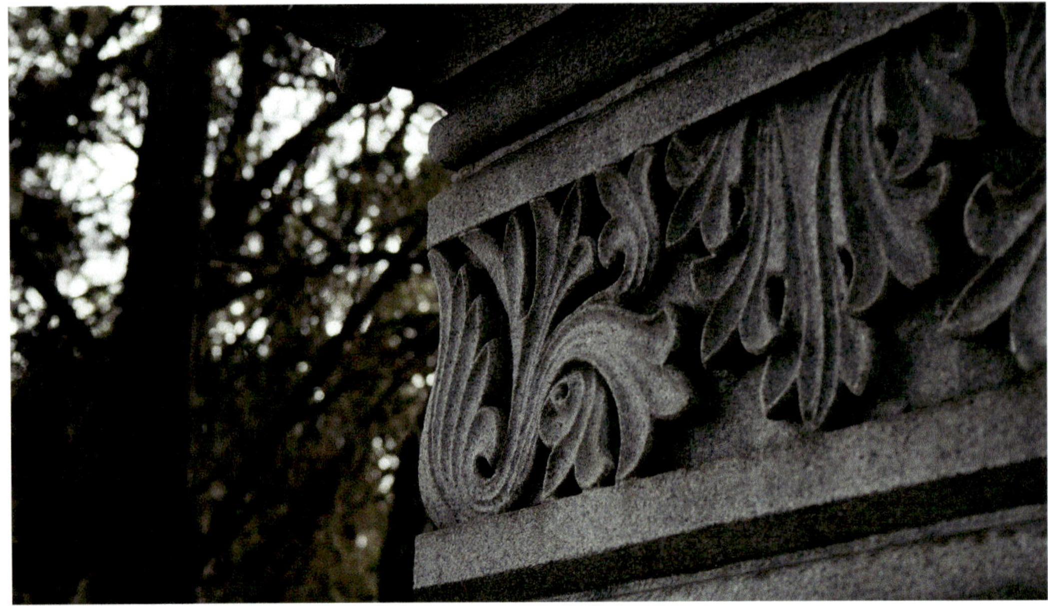

Carved in stone, the intricate scrollwork of this monument stands as a tribute to craftsmanship and memory.

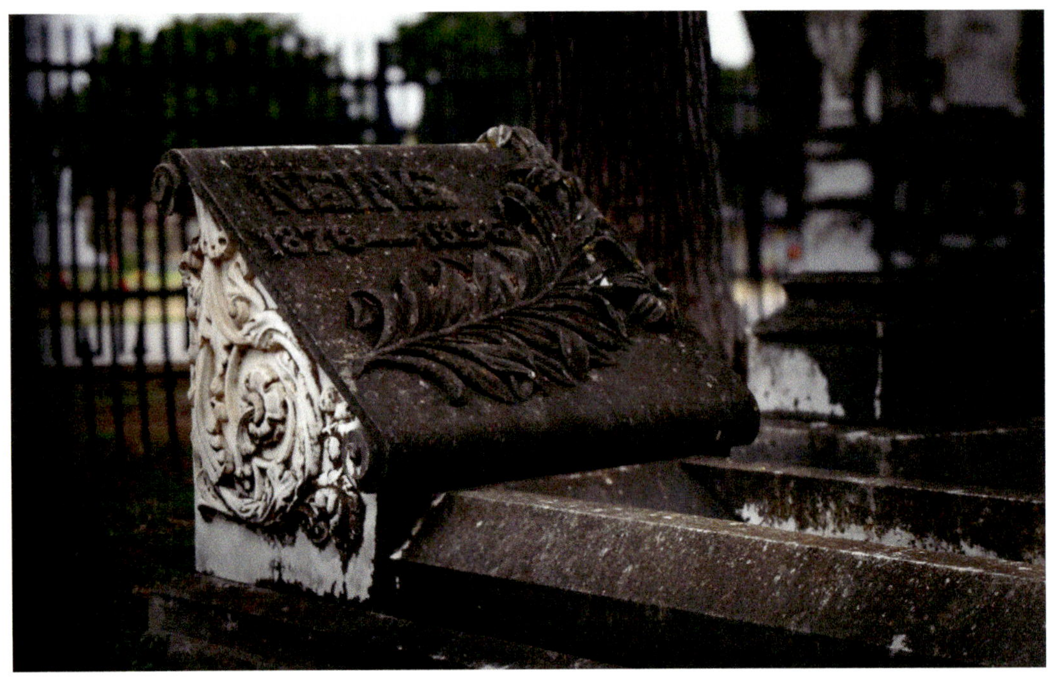

This unique headstone is a stunning example of intricate craftsmanship, blending elegance with solemnity. The sculpted acanthus leaves curl gracefully across the slanted surface, symbolizing enduring life and remembrance.

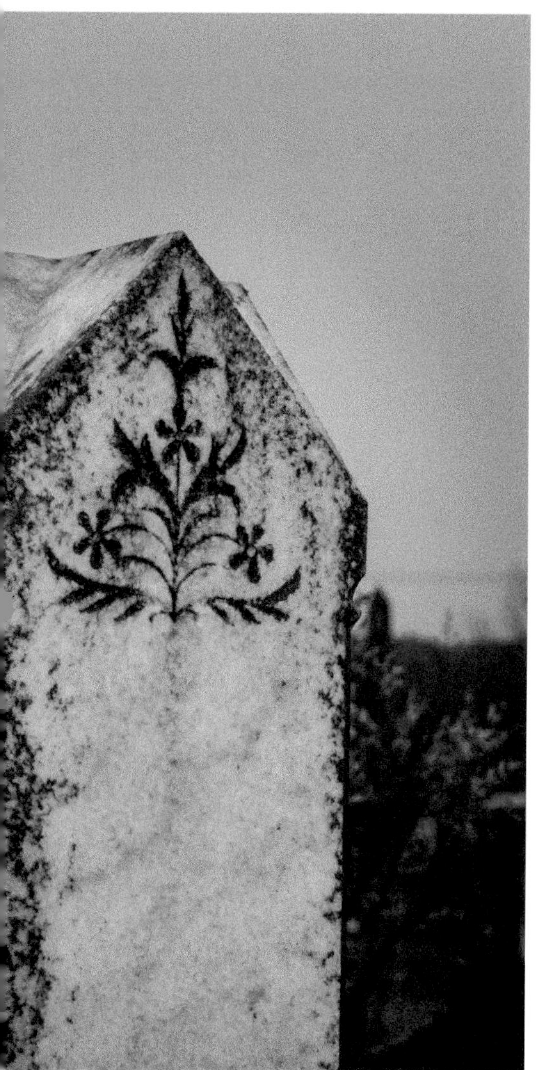

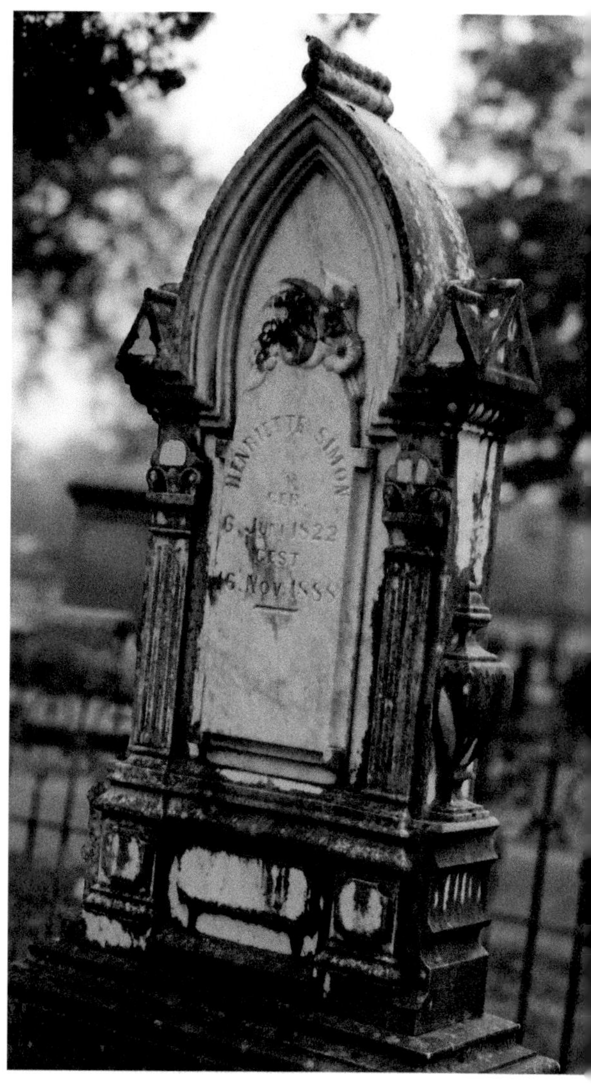

Above left: Faded floral engravings bloom through time, etched in stone and softened by nature's touch.

Above right: A Gothic-style monument, embellished with intricate floral engravings and ornate finials, continues to stand tall.

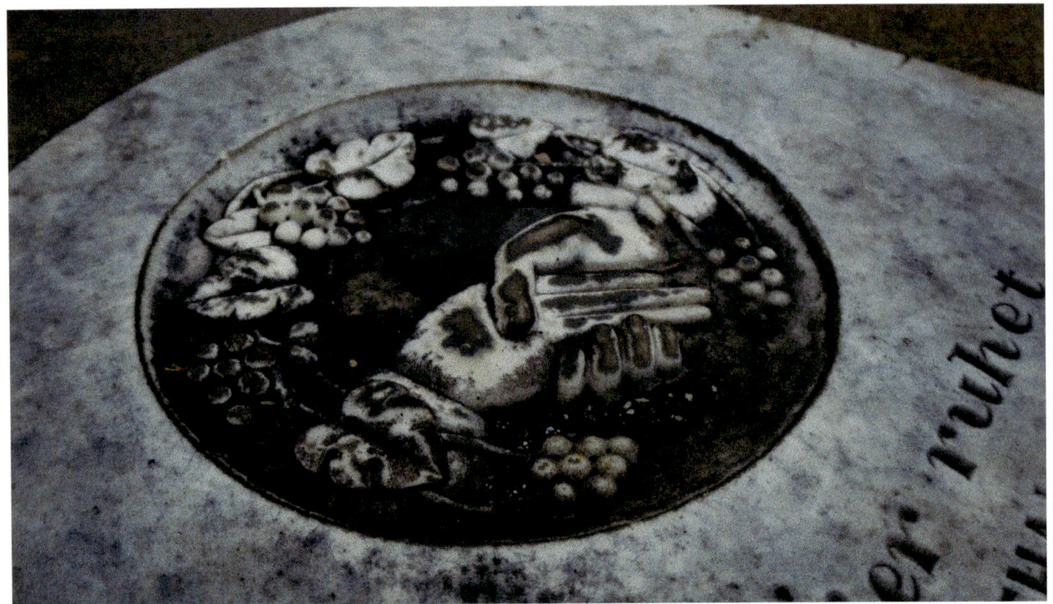

Time's embrace lingers in stone, with clasped hands frozen in farewell, entwined with vines that whisper of eternity.

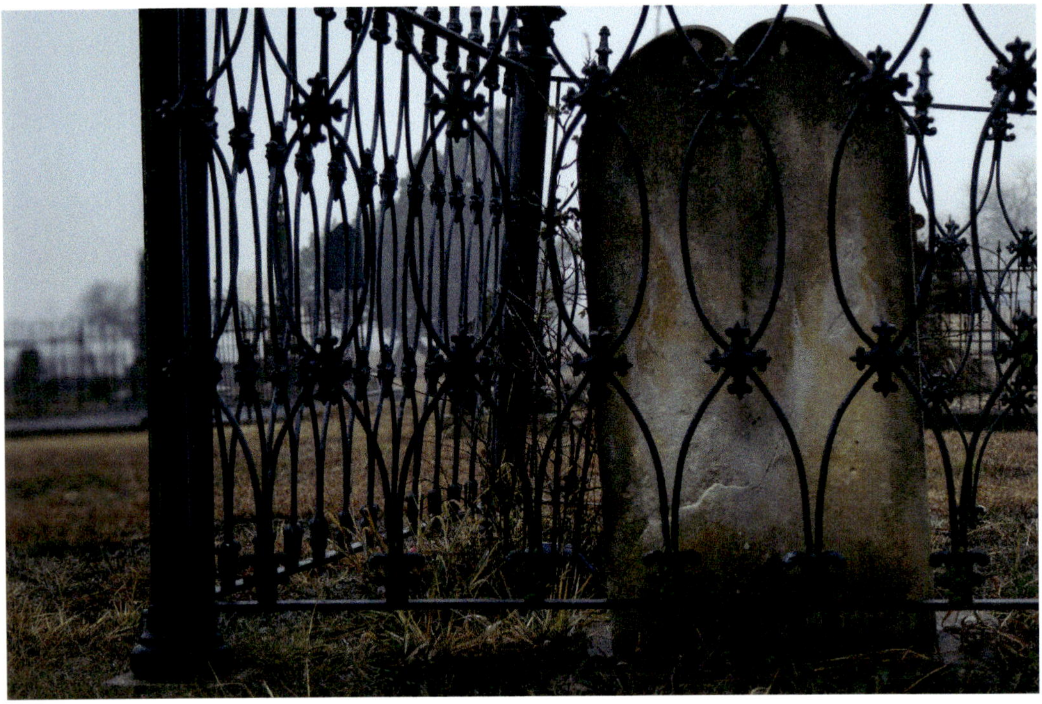

Bound by iron, embraced by time, weathered stone and rusted bars stand as silent keepers of forgotten names.

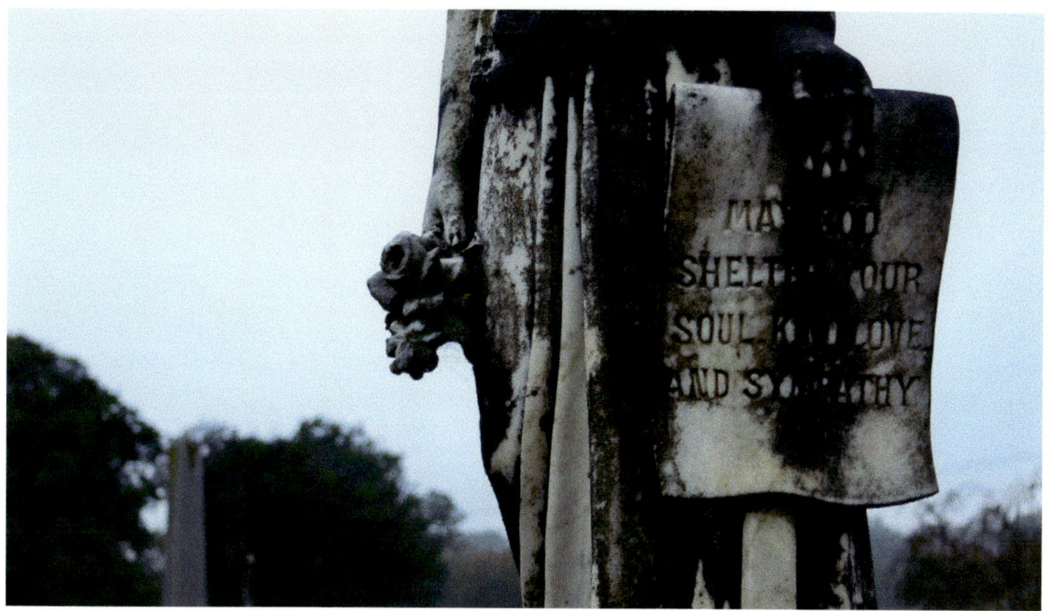

A stone figure holds a delicate bouquet and a message of love and sympathy. Moss clings to her flowing robes and fading inscription.

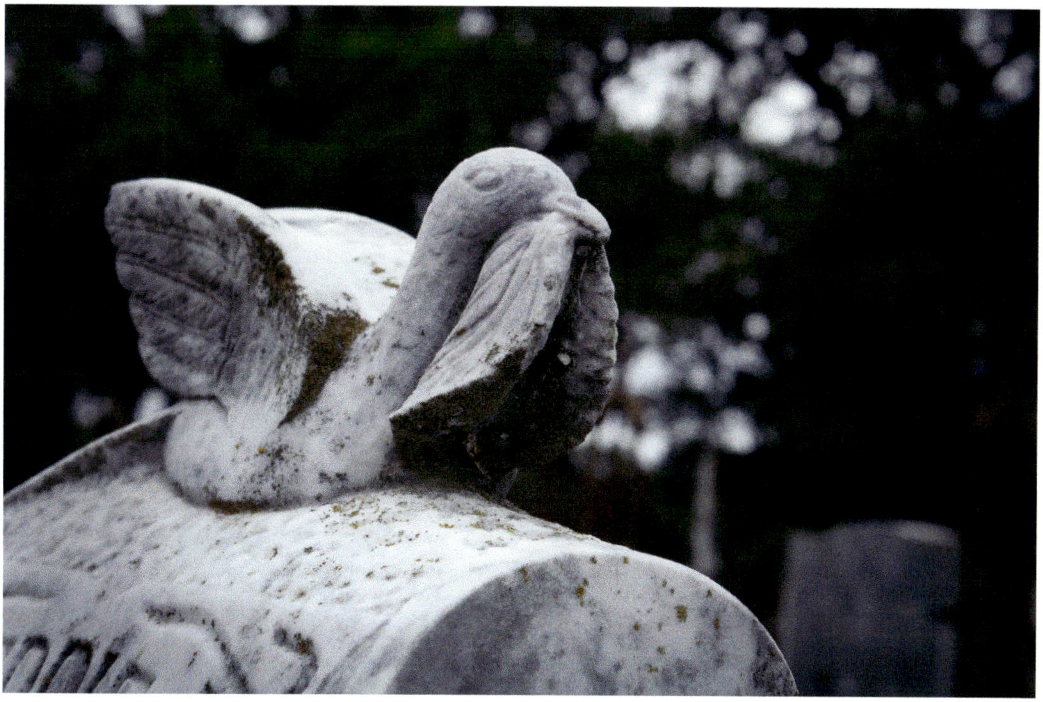

A weathered marble dove, clutching a gentle branch in its beak, perches atop a gravestone, its wings slightly raised as if caught in an eternal moment of flight.

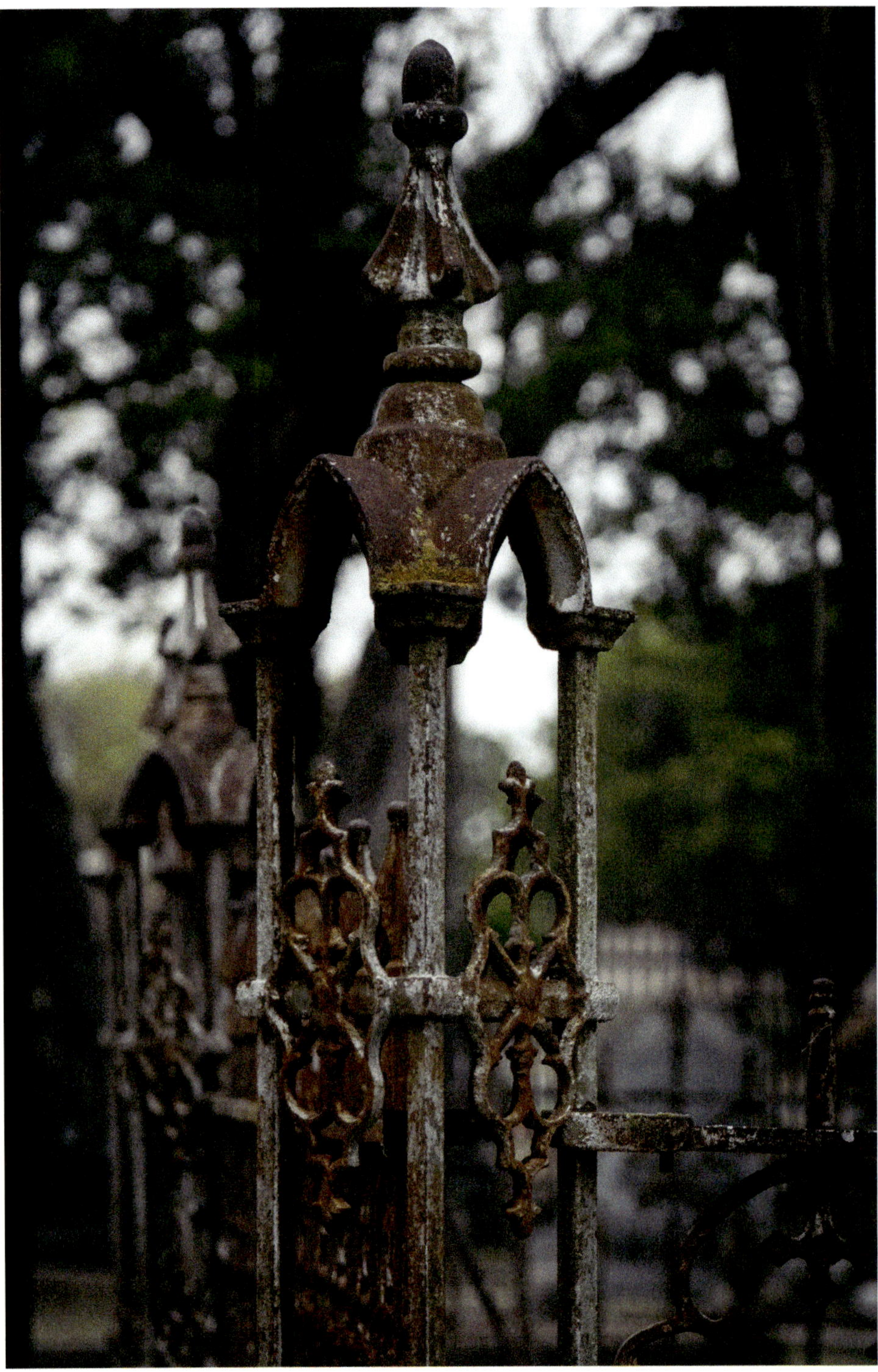

Ornate gothic-inspired patterns weave through rusted bars, their delicate details softened by corrosion.

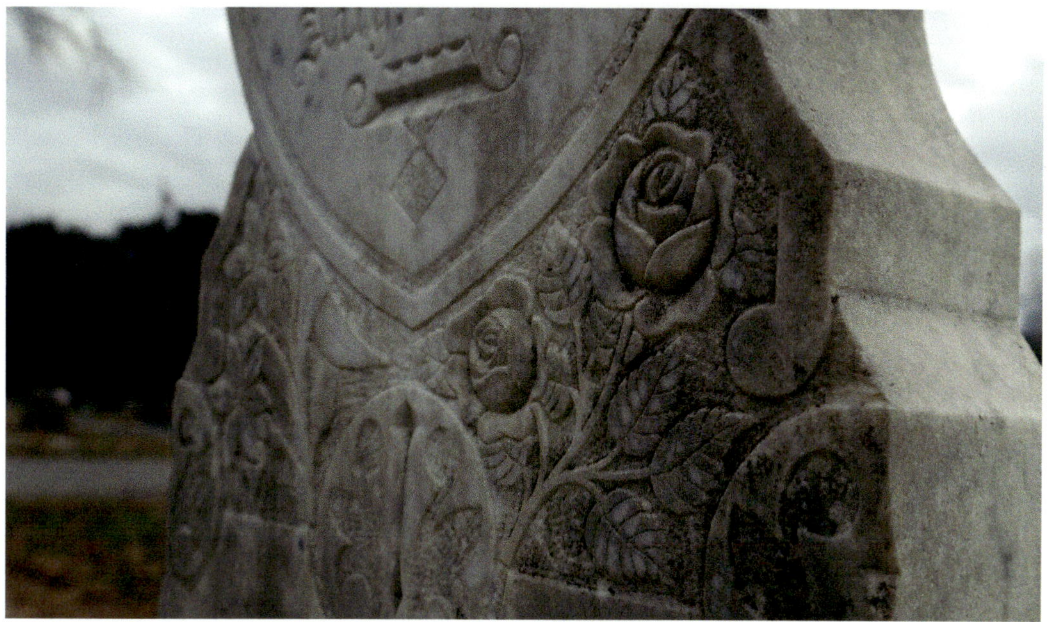

Above: Intricate vine motifs intertwine with flourishing leaves, each chiseled detail demonstrating the artisan's skill.

Right: The ornate finial, with its delicate curves and ridges, was once a proud decorative element, now worn by the elements, pitted and textured with corrosion.

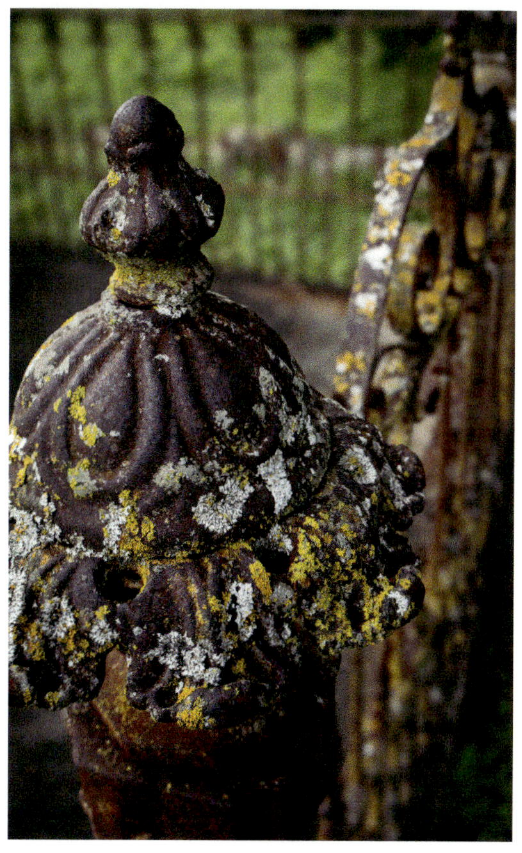

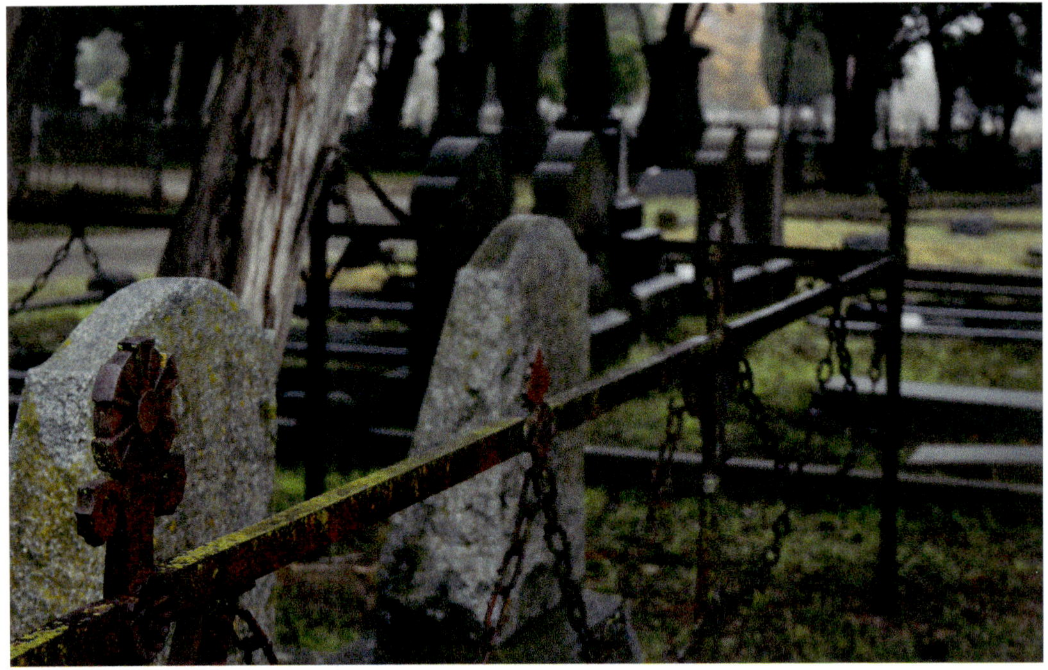

Rust creeps, stones weather, but the chains remain locked, holding fast to a past that refuses to be undone.

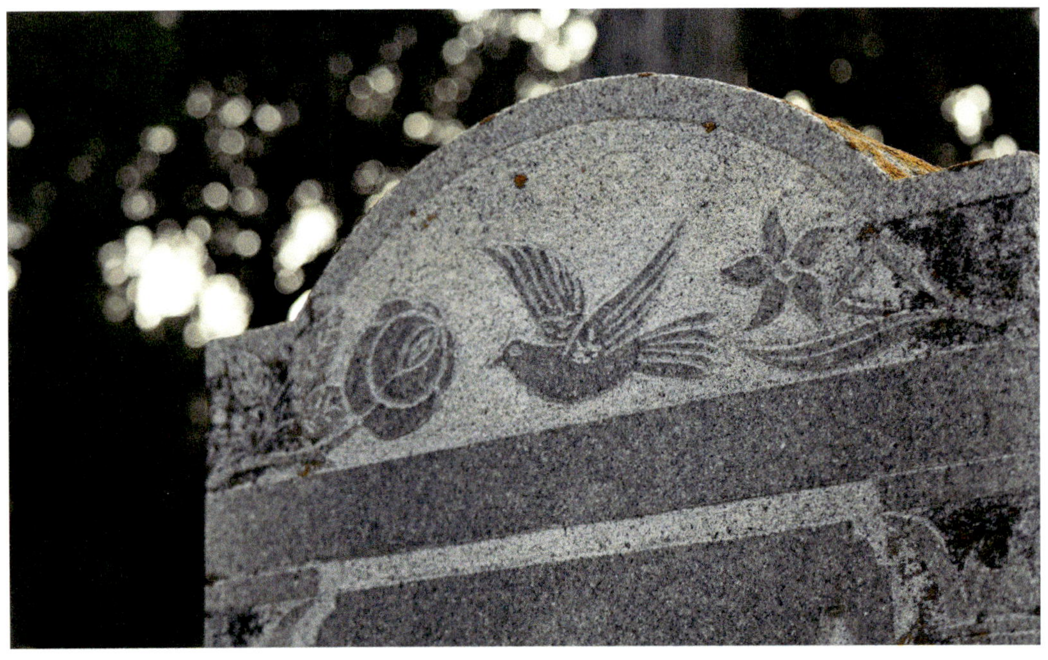

A delicate engraving of a bird in flight, framed by roses and wildflowers, graces this headstone.

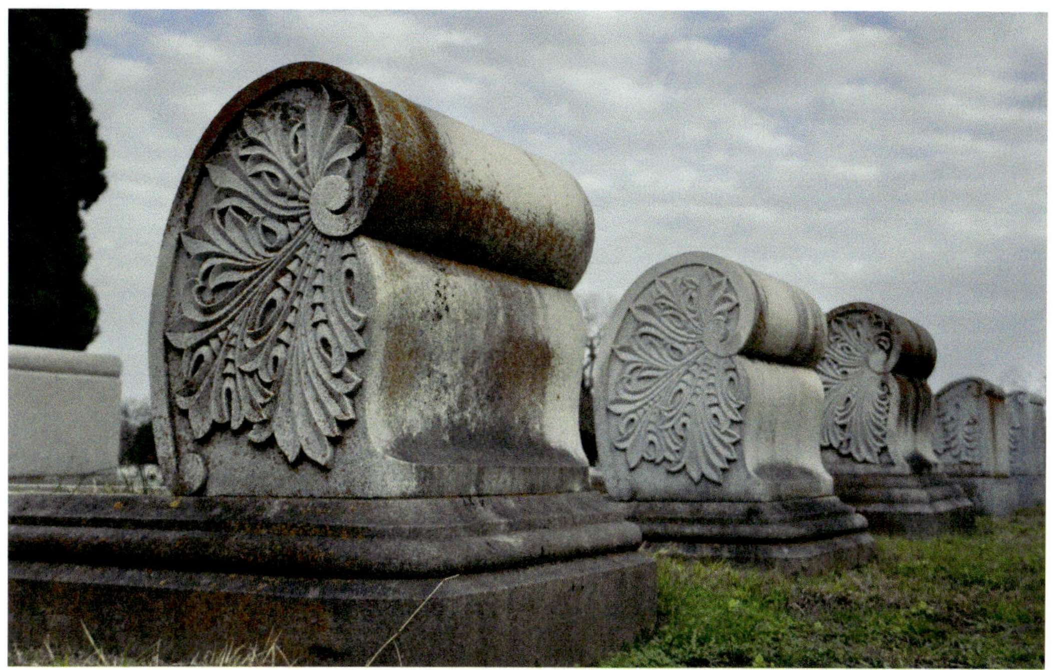

These headstones, lined up in succession and each shaped in the form of a scroll, embody a sense of timeless artistry and symbolism.

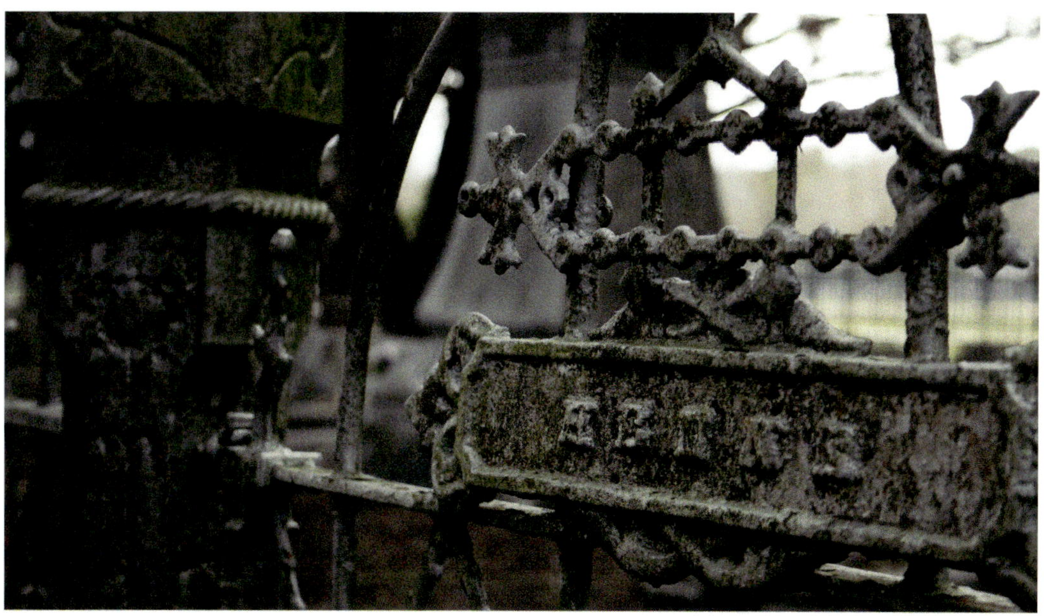

Cloaked in time's decay, this rusted iron fence bears intricate gothic-style details, from its delicate rosettes to the ornate, spiked latticework. The nameplate, worn and corroded, holds only faint traces of its original inscription.

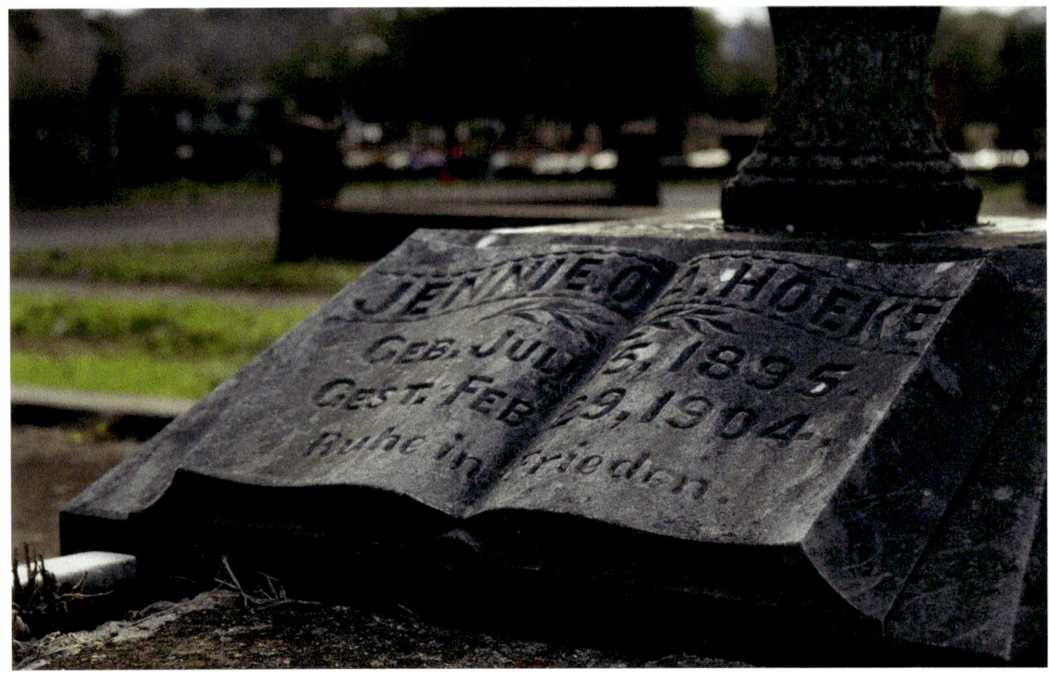

This unique headstone is shaped like an open book, symbolizing a life story that has come to an end. The deep, bold engravings of the name and dates remain legible despite the passage of time.

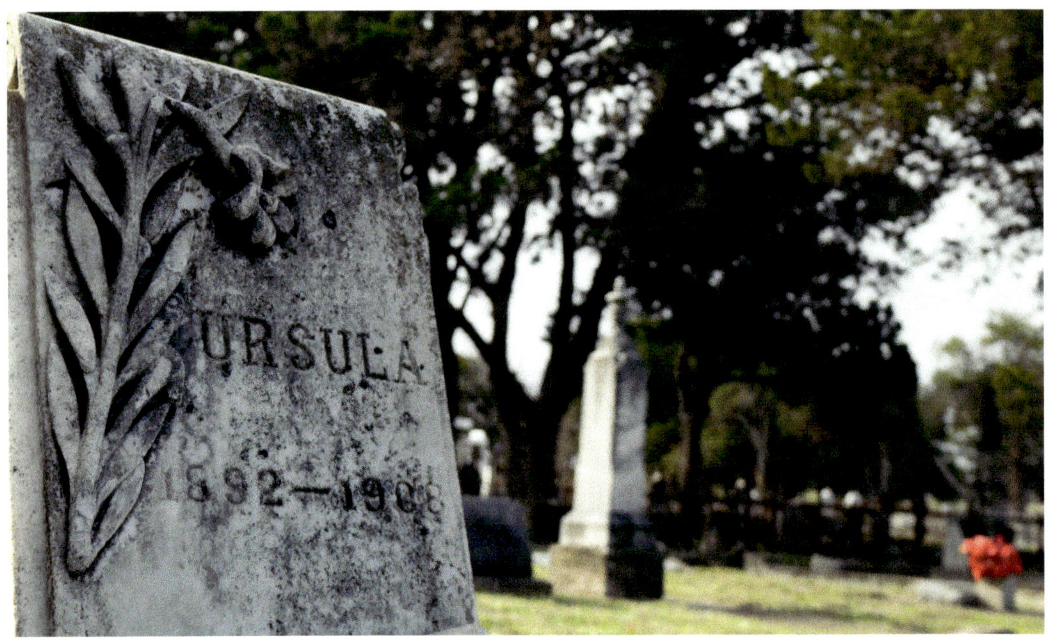

Time and the elements have left their mark on this headstone embellished with a single, delicate lily. Time added a textured patina that only deepens its quiet beauty.

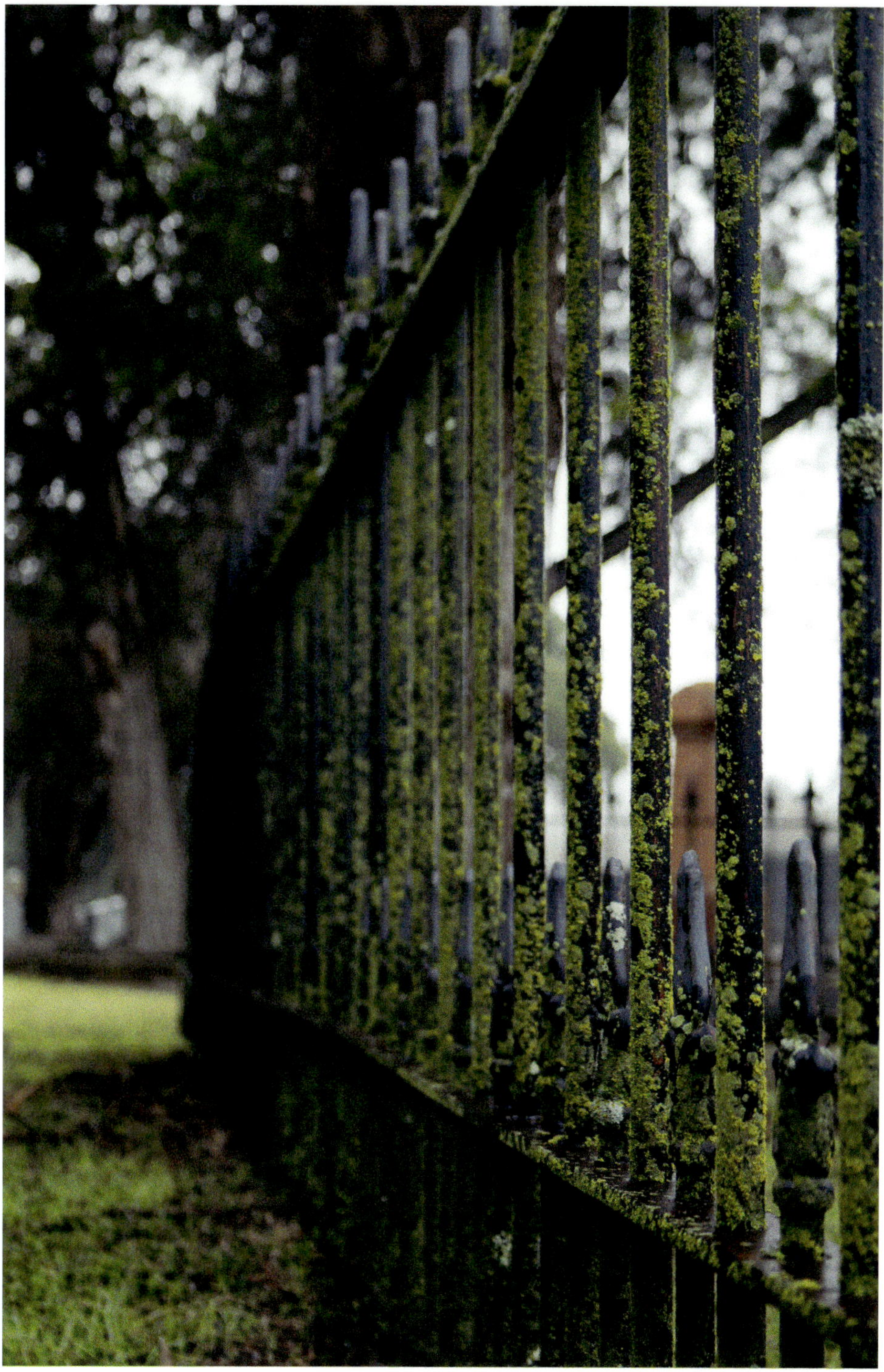

A simple yet elegant iron fence, its pointed finials standing in quiet vigilance, marking the boundary between past and present.

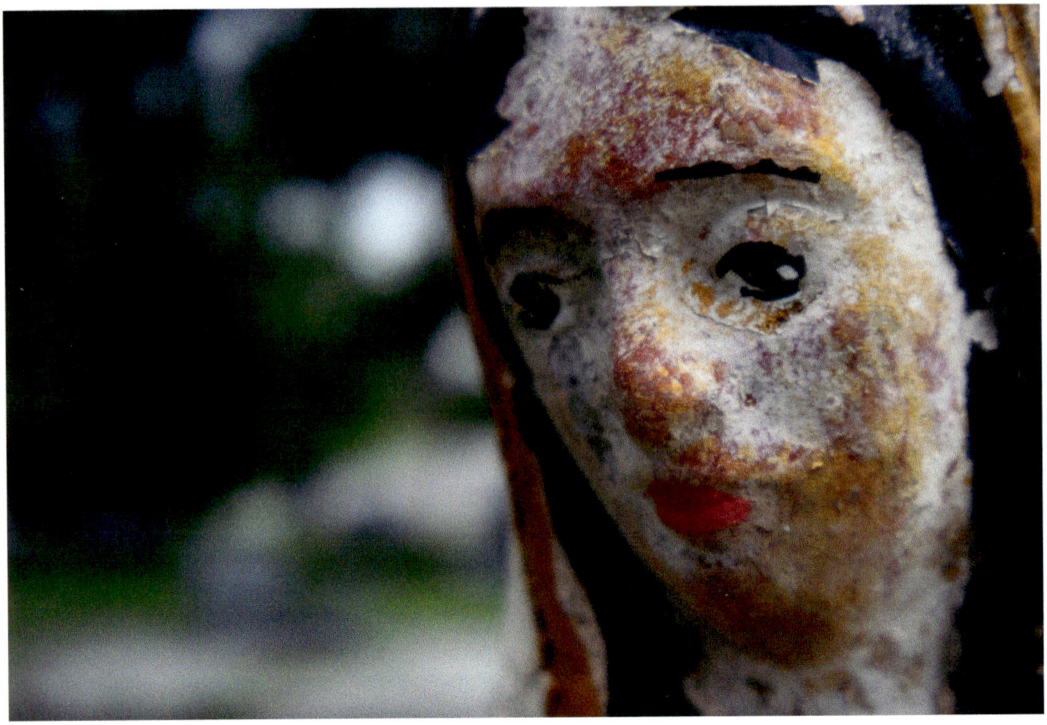

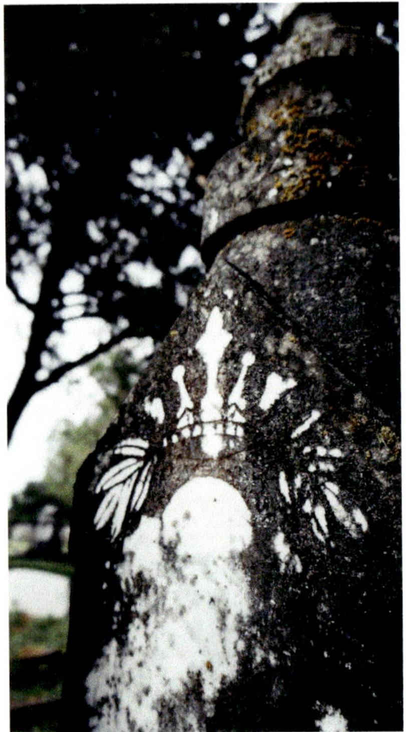

Above: This close-up captures the weathered face of a painted statue, its contours faded with age.

Left: The once-pristine engraving, possibly depicting a radiant sunburst or a celestial crown, is now a ghostly silhouette.

Right: This headstone is a striking display of intricate craftsmanship, its surface adorned with layers of carved floral motifs and delicate wreath-like embellishments.

Below: A rusted cemetery gate from 1876, its nameplate worn and laced with moss, stands as a quiet sentinel of memory.

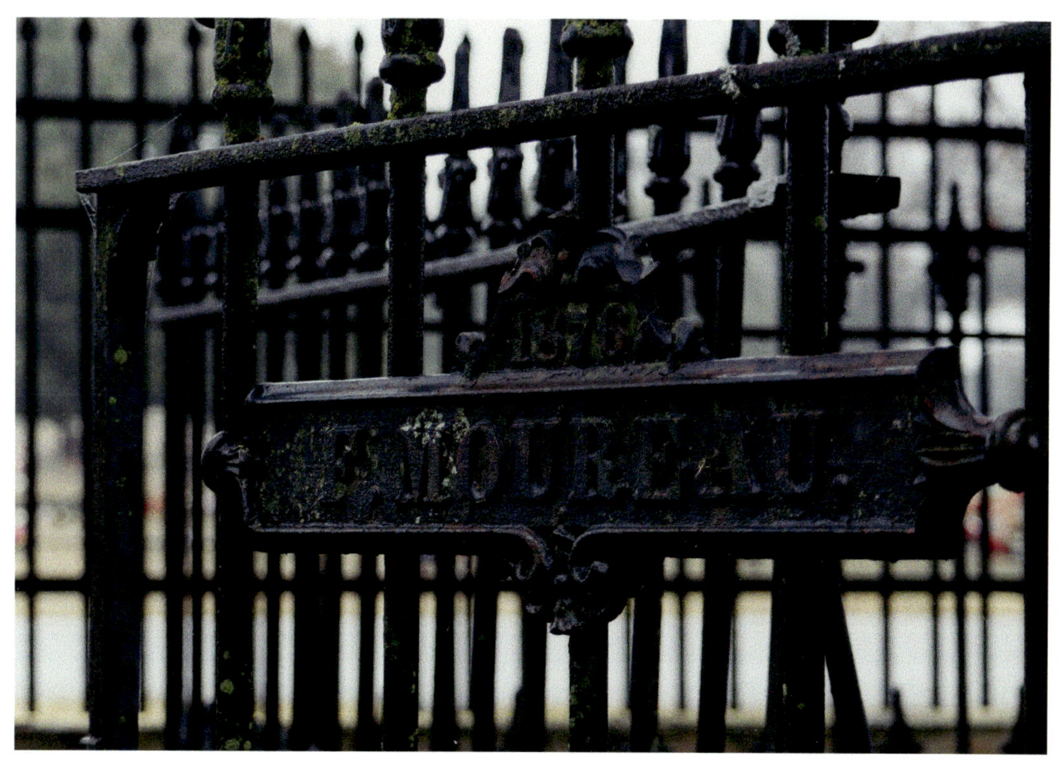

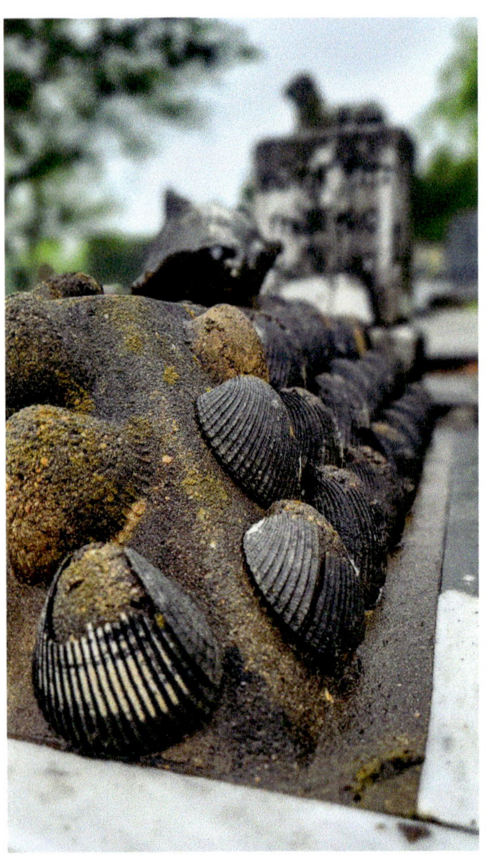

Left: Seashells fused with time, forming a tribute to a life tied to the sea. A monument where nature and memory become one.

Below: This photograph captures a close-up of an aged stone carving, displaying a hand gently grasping a small bouquet of flowers.

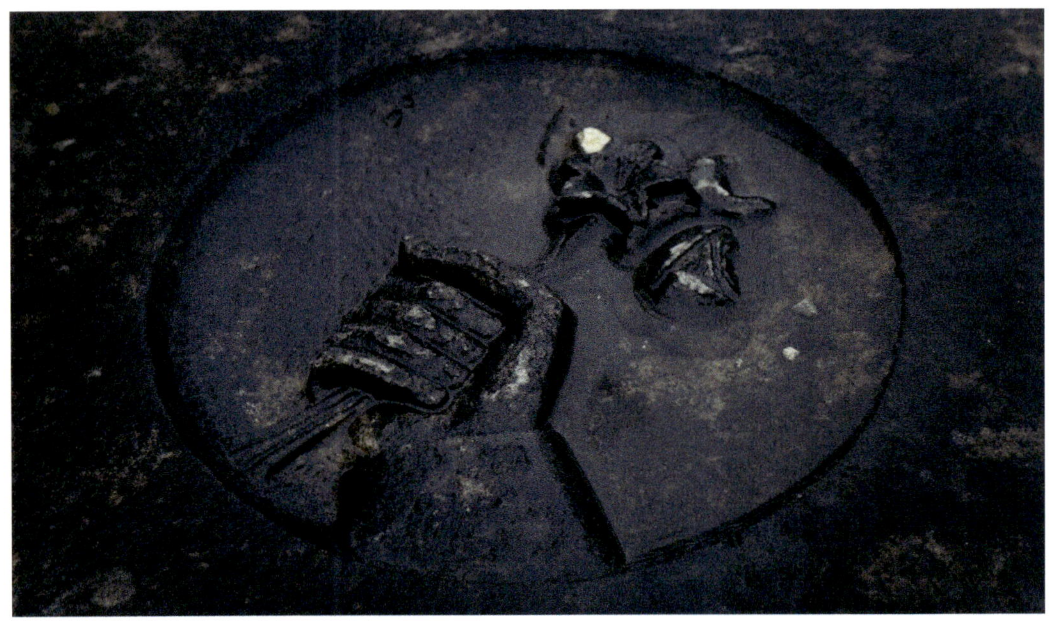

Right: This image captures the striking details of a rusted iron finial atop an aged cemetery fence. Its shape, reminiscent of a Gothic or Victorian design, adds a sense of solemn grandeur to the scene.

Below: The relief work on this headstone features delicate lilies of the valley blossoms, their tiny, bell-shaped blooms arranged along gracefully curved stems.

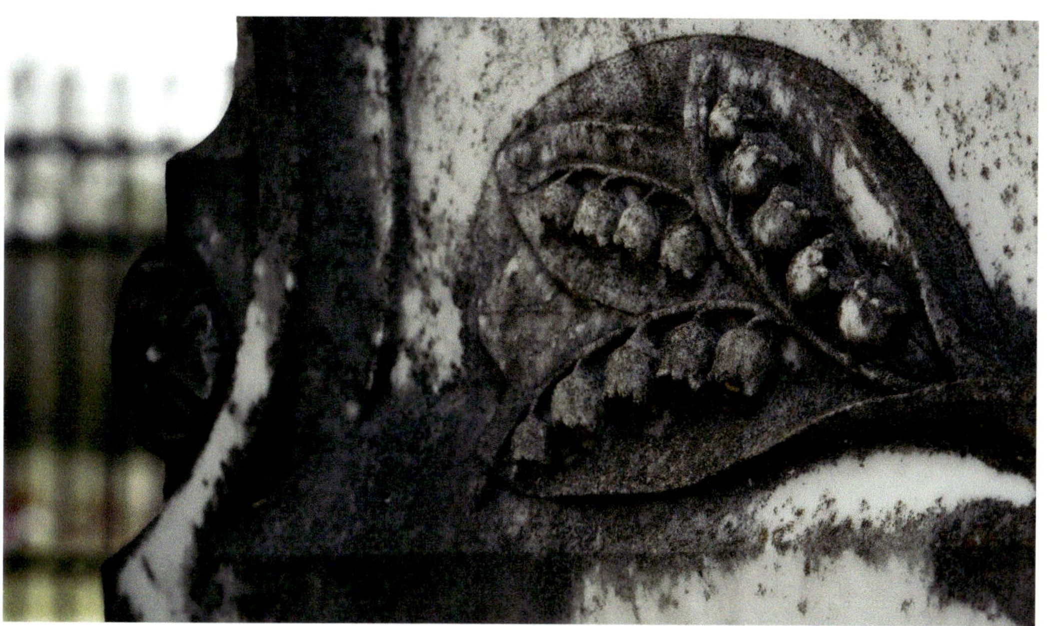

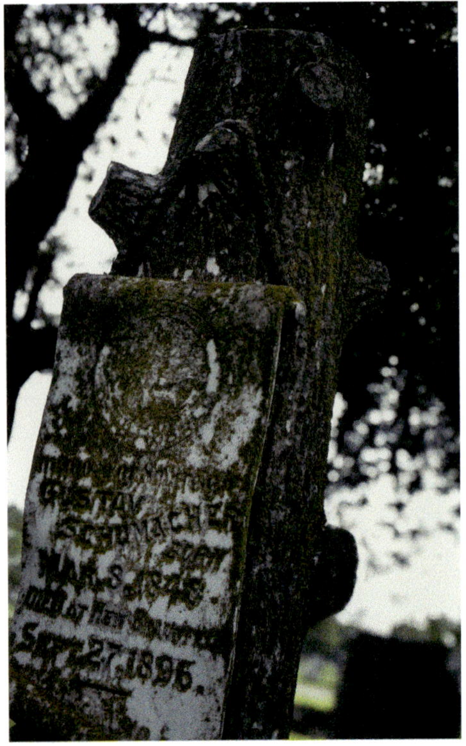

This monument, shaped like a tree trunk, serves as a poignant symbol of life ending too soon.

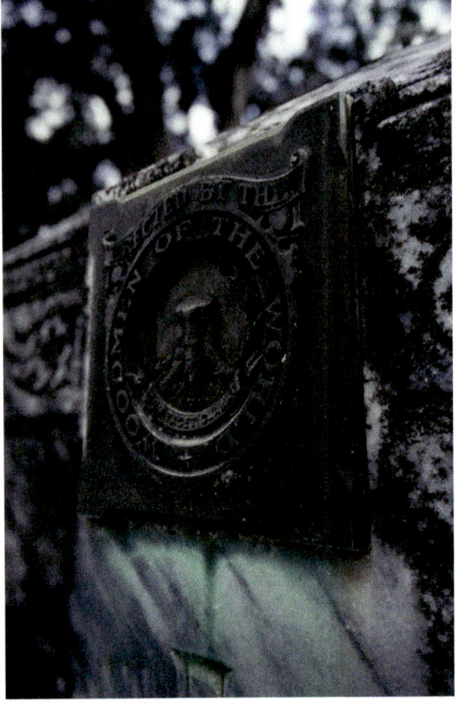

Woodmen of the World is a fraternal benefit society established in 1890, recognized for offering life insurance and community service. Historically, it provided unique tree trunk-shaped headstones for members, representing strength and remembrance.

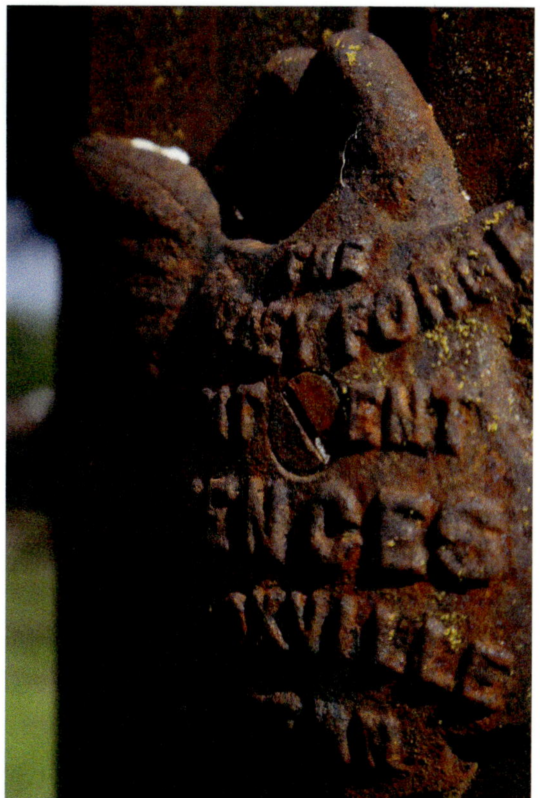

Right: A rusted eagle emblem, clinging to the fence once proudly marked.

Below: This gravestone features an elegant, deeply carved floral relief of lily of the valley drooping across the name "Schleyer," typically signifying mourning.

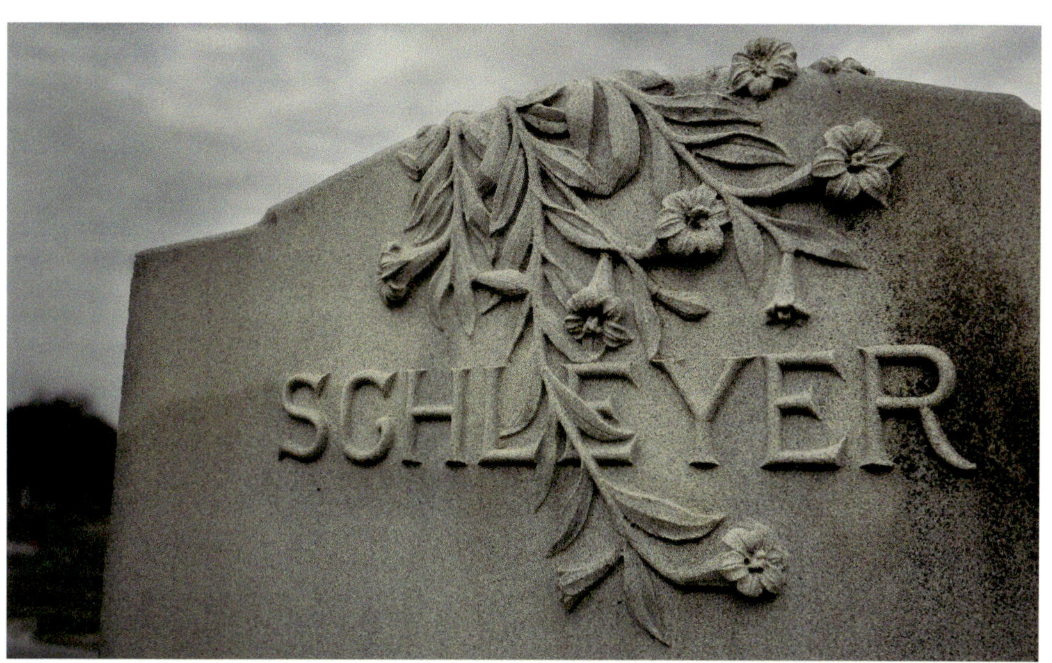

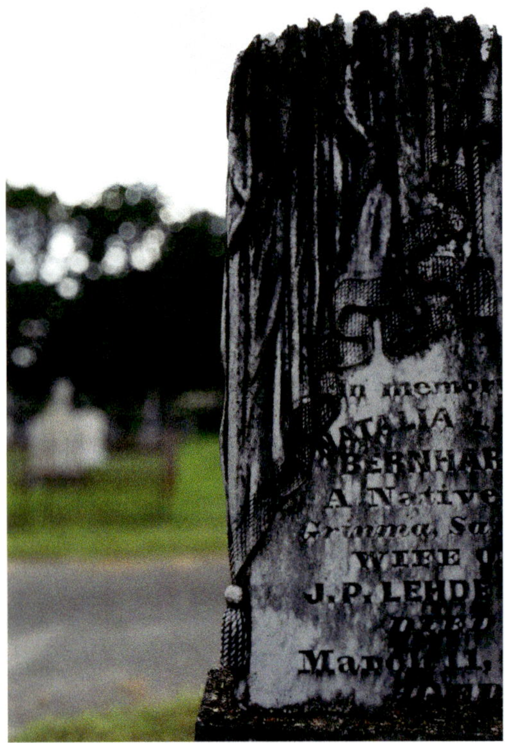

Left: This tombstone features an exquisitely detailed, draped cloth motif, an age-old funerary symbol representing the veil between life and death.

Below: A rusted iron fence adorned with ornate crosses stretches toward the horizon.

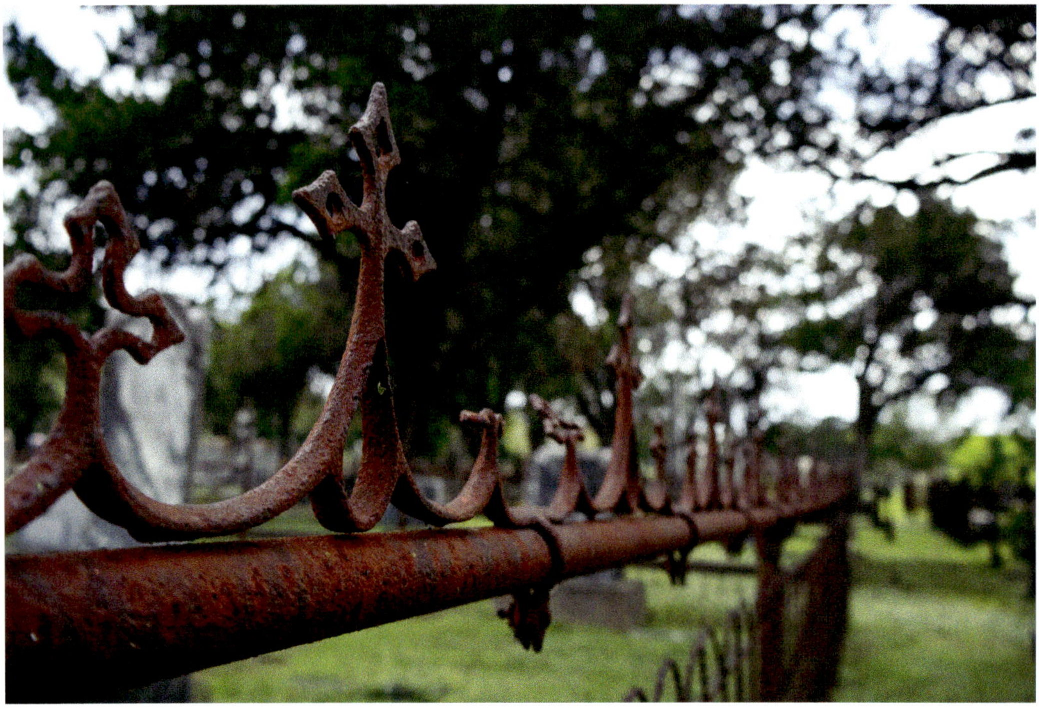

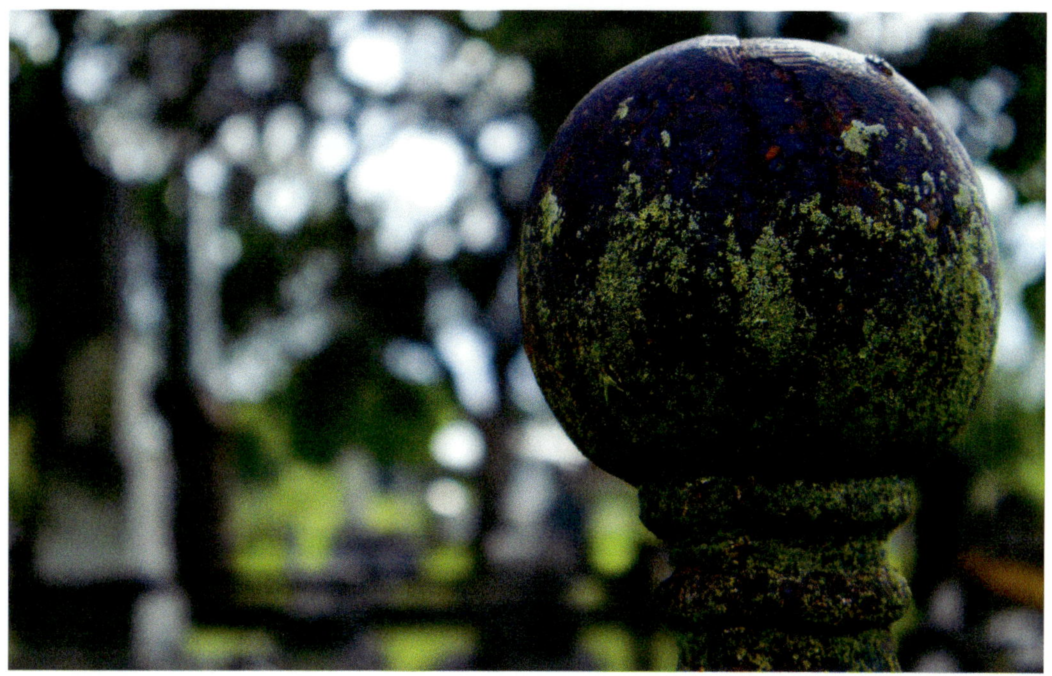

Time and nature entwine as a rusted iron finial, draped in lichen, stands as a quiet sentinel against the blurred backdrop of weathered gravestones and whispering trees.

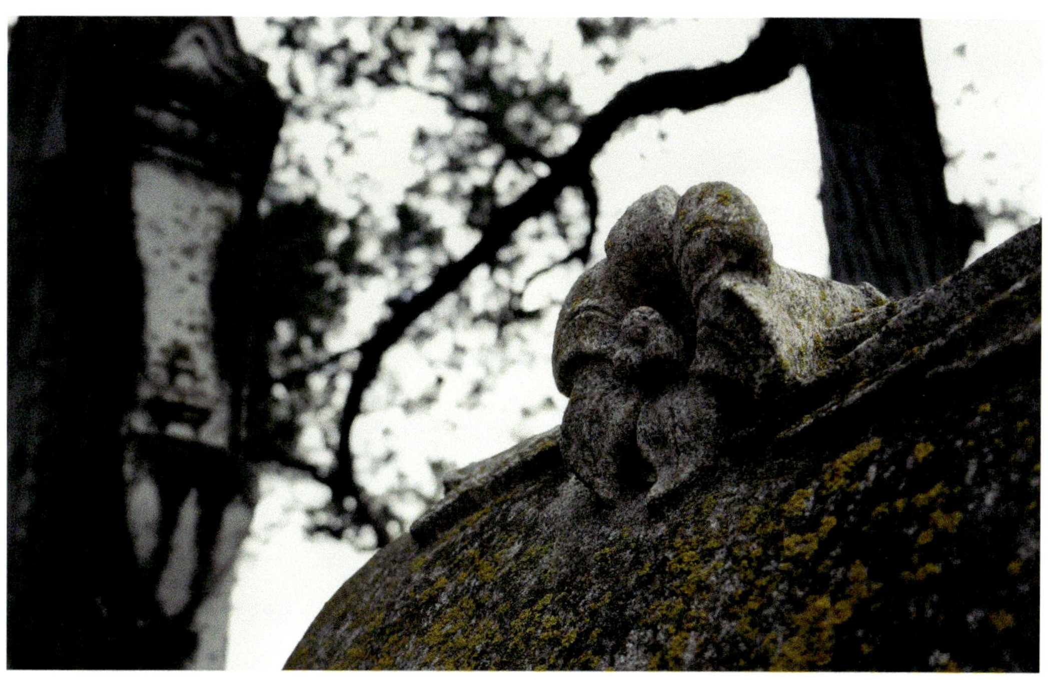

A gracefully aged stone carving of a flower crowns this monument.

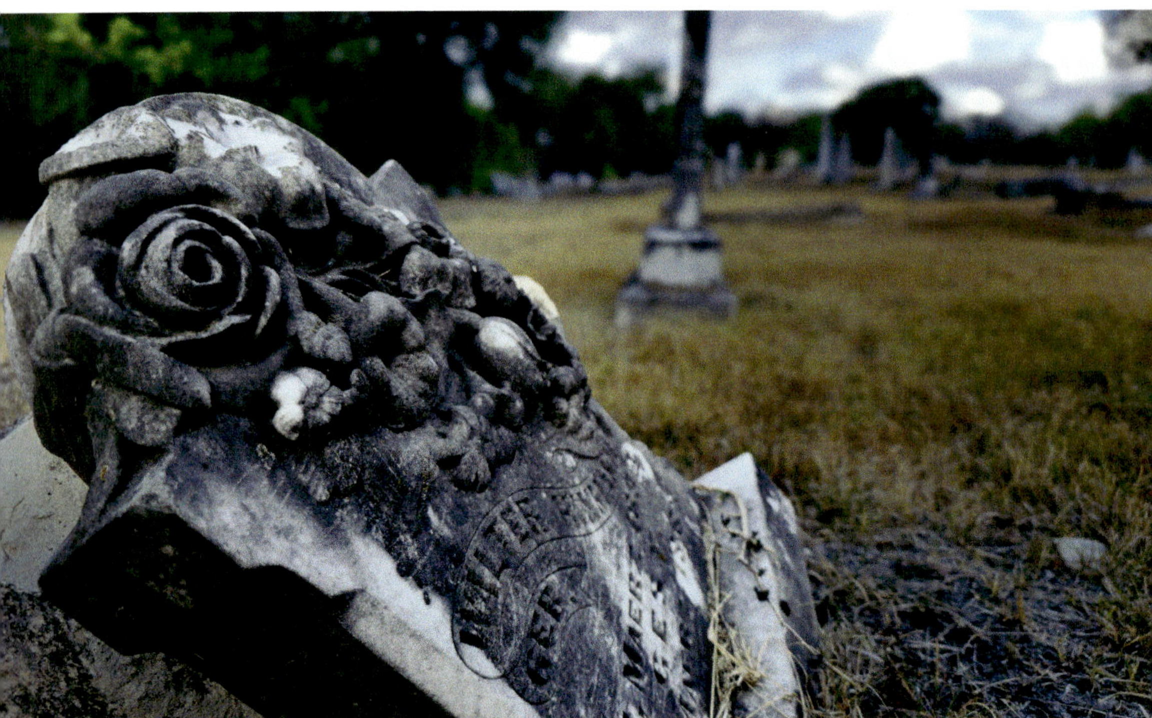

Time bows even the strongest stone, like this tombstone. Sinking into the earth, it displays beautifully detailed carved flowers.

5
TRACES OF LOVE

The Mementos Left Behind

Among the headstones and statues of New Braunfels' cemeteries lie small but powerful reminders of love and loss, tokens left behind by those who still remember. Angel statues stand in quiet vigil, their once-pristine forms softened by rain and time. Artificial flowers, once bright and full of life, now lay brittle and colorless, yet their presence remains a testament to devotion.

Though weathered by time, these mementos tell stories that refuse to fade. Some are carefully placed by visitors who return repeatedly, while others have stood for years, slowly surrendering to the elements. Yet, even as nature reclaims them, they endure in their fragility, their fleeting presence, and their deeply human truth.

In this chapter, we explore the quiet beauty of these offerings, the way they withstand time and weather, and the universal longing to leave something behind for those who can no longer hold them.

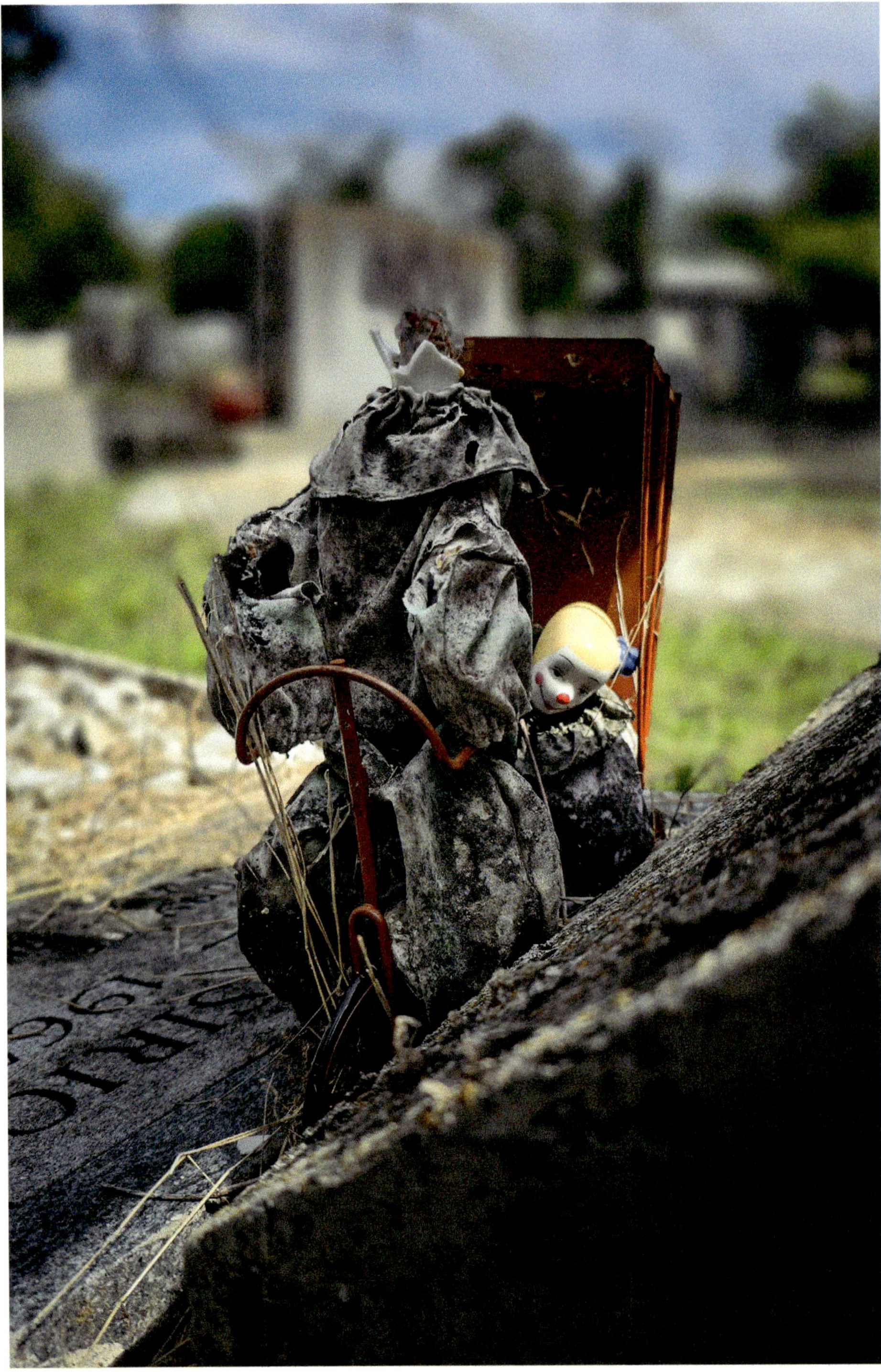

A tattered and weathered clown figurine slumps against a headstone, its once vibrant fabric now decayed and discolored by time.

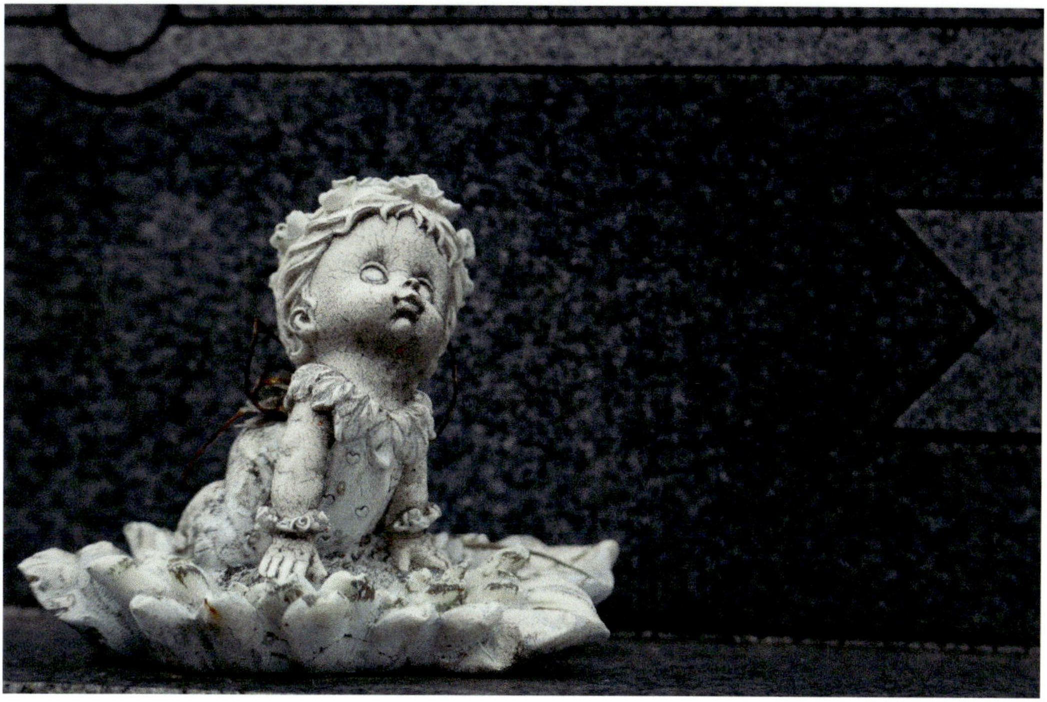

A weathered porcelain cherub gazes upward.

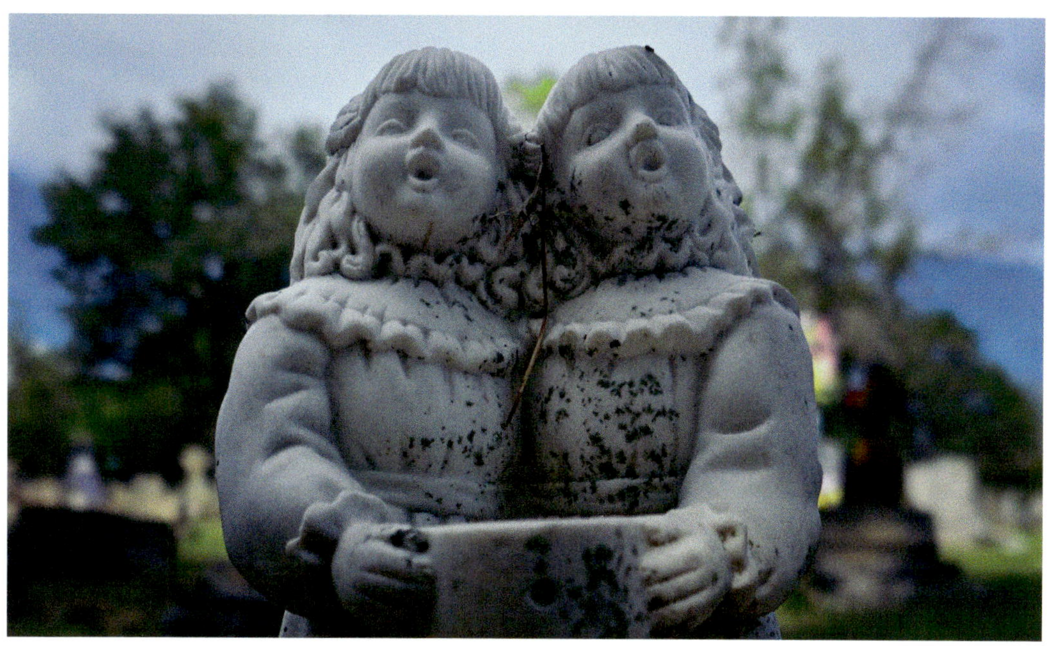

This eerie yet endearing sculpture features two twin girls, side by side, holding a small object between them.

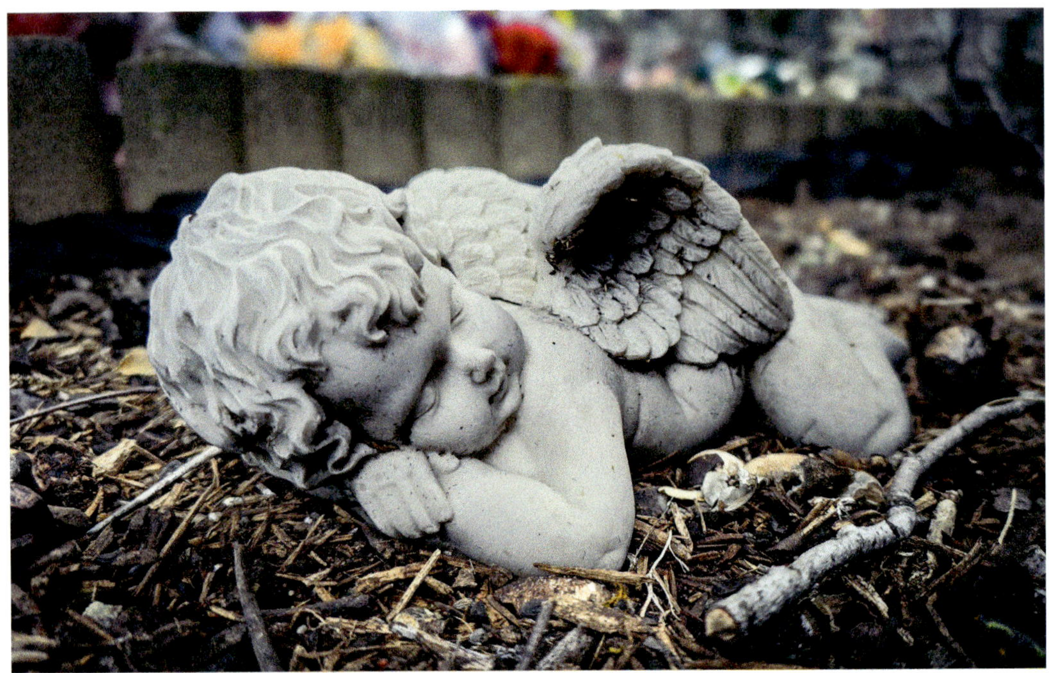

Nestled among scattered twigs and decaying leaves, a weathered stone cherub rests in eternal slumber.

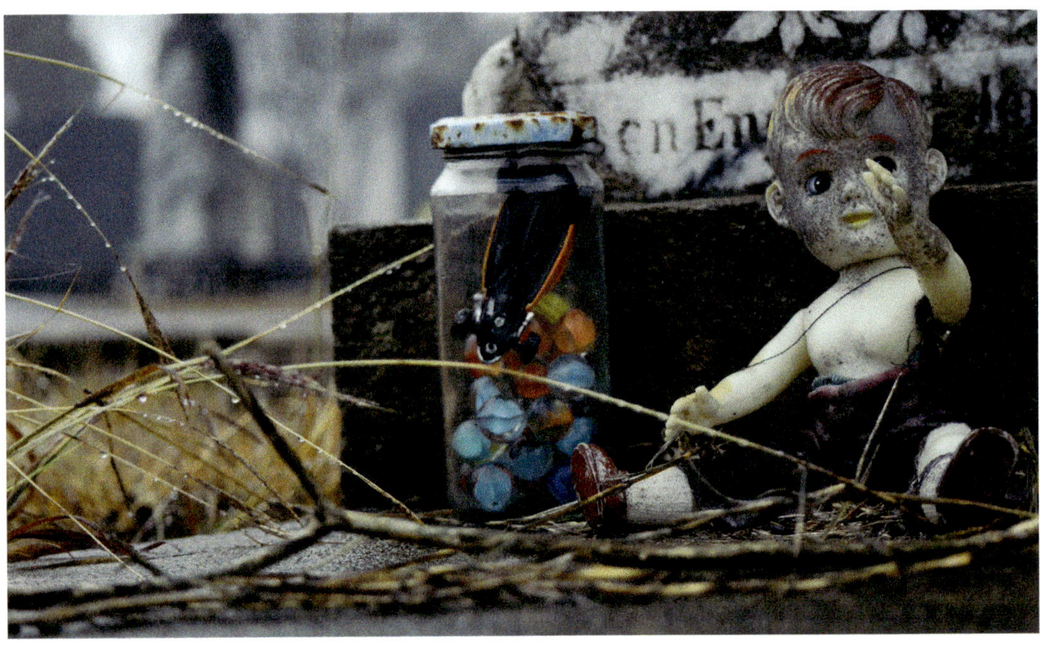

A weathered doll with tattered clothes sits against a moss-covered grave, its outstretched arm frozen in time.

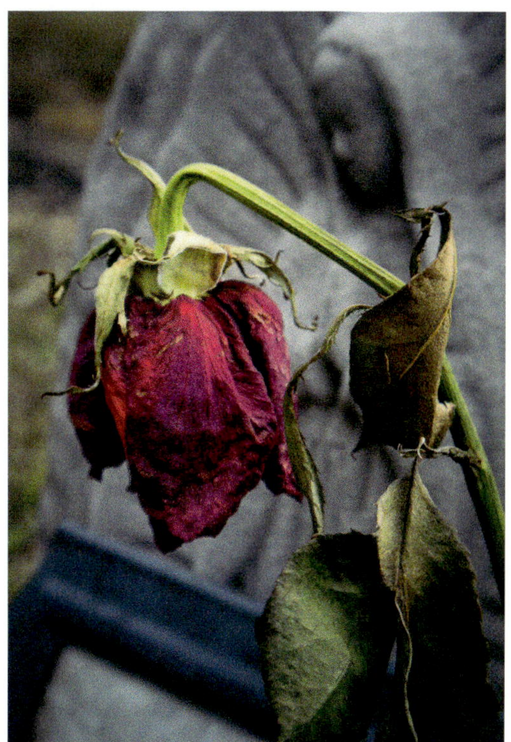

Right: A withered rose droops, its deep crimson petals now tinged with decay.

Below: A broken porcelain angel kneels on a gravestone.

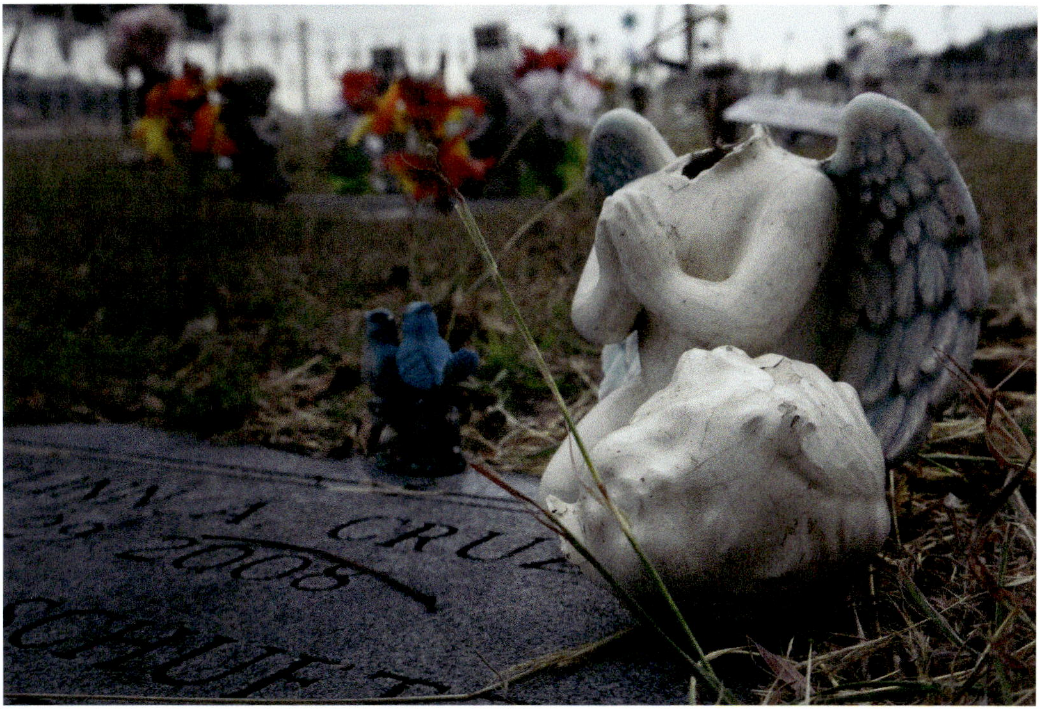

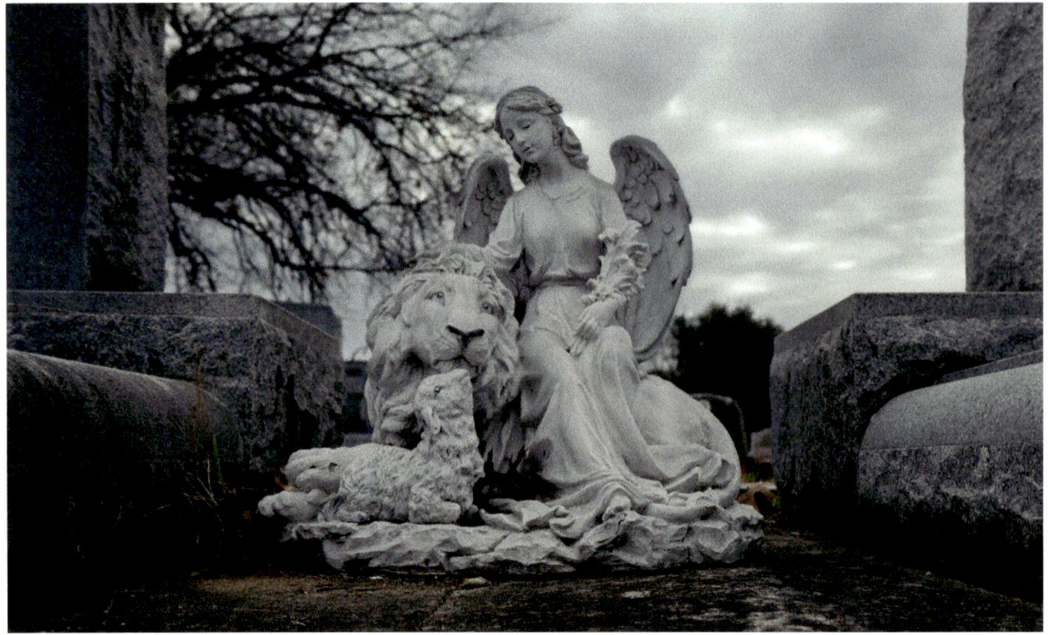

An angel kneels in quiet grace, her hand resting gently upon the head of a lion. A lamb sits at their feet, completing this sacred trio as symbols of peace, strength, and divine protection.

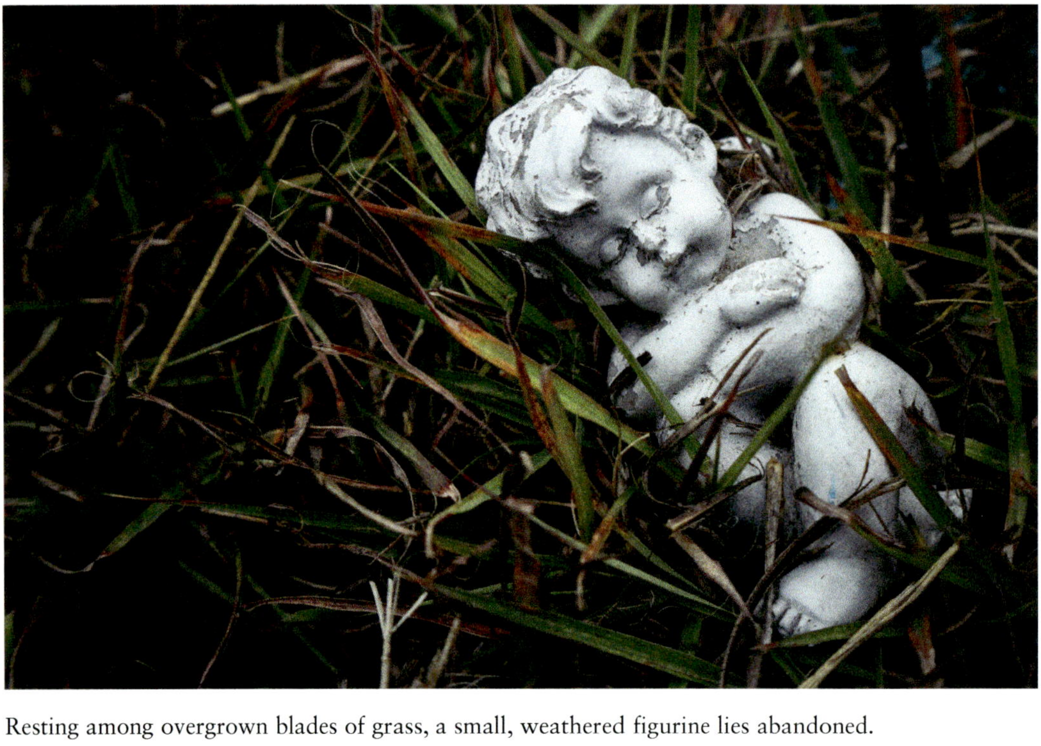

Resting among overgrown blades of grass, a small, weathered figurine lies abandoned.

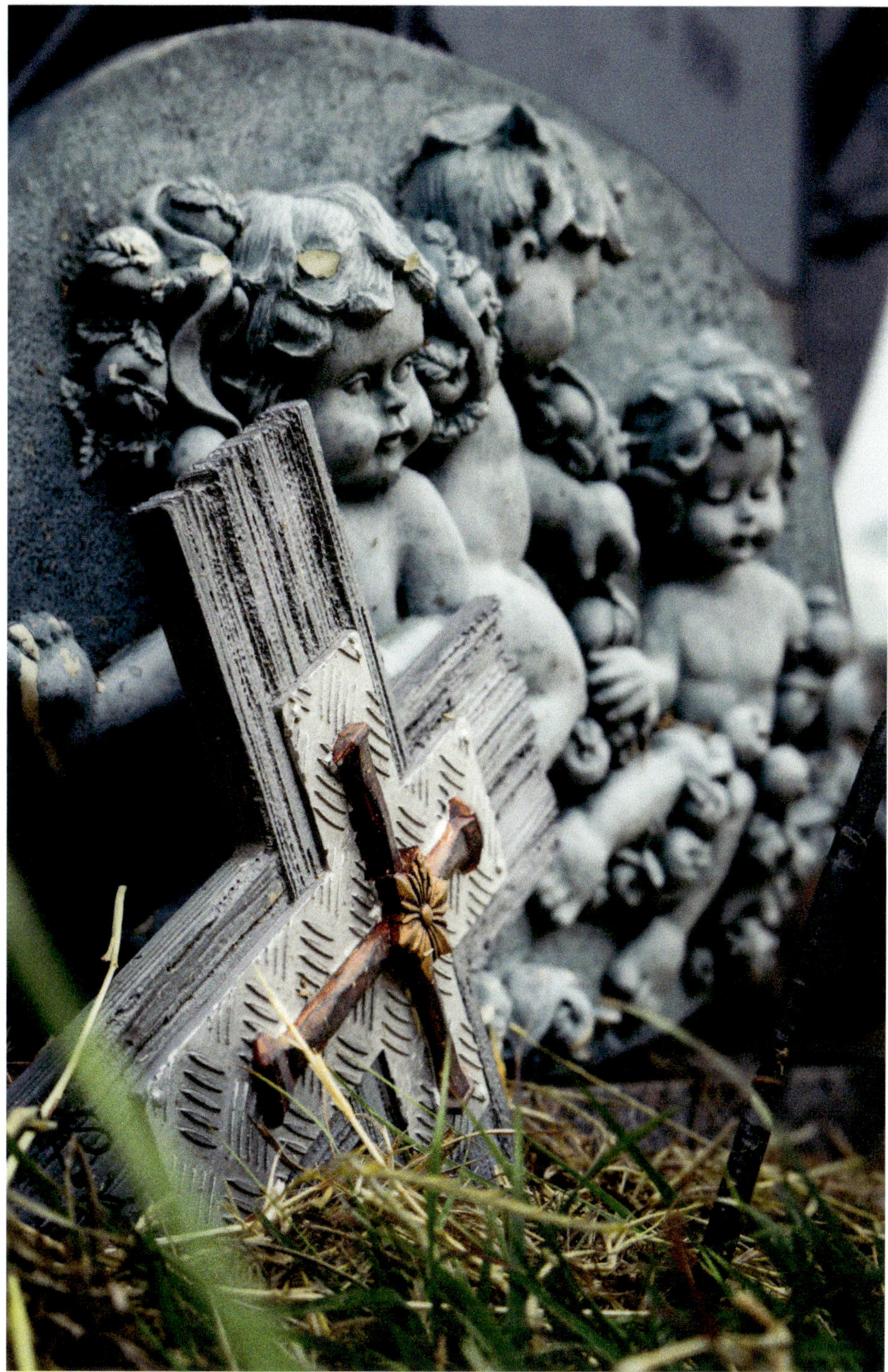

A cross rests among overgrown grass. Behind it, a stone relief of cherubs, worn and chipped, stands as a silent reminder of innocence and loss.

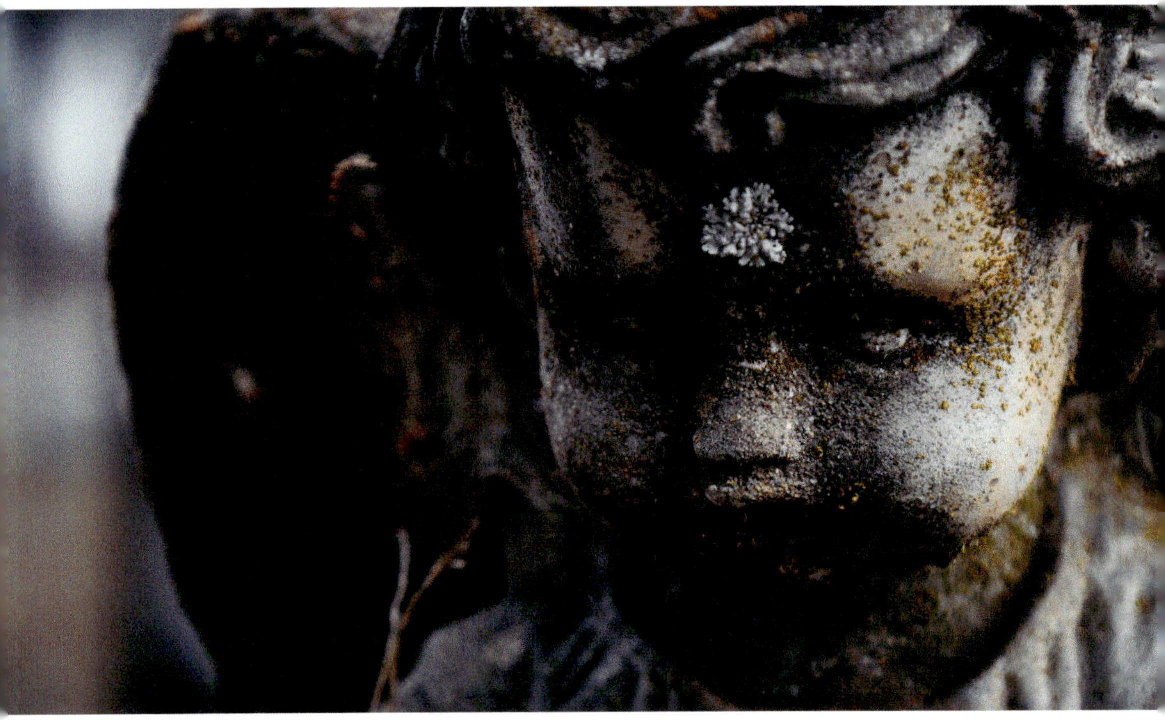

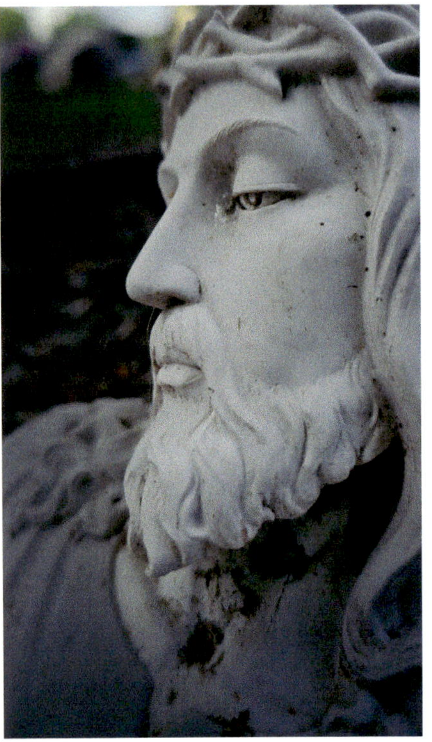

Above: Though much time has passed, this melancholic angel remains, unchanging, untouched, forgotten by all but nature.

Left: A close-up of a weathered stone statue depicting Jesus, wearing a crown of thorns.

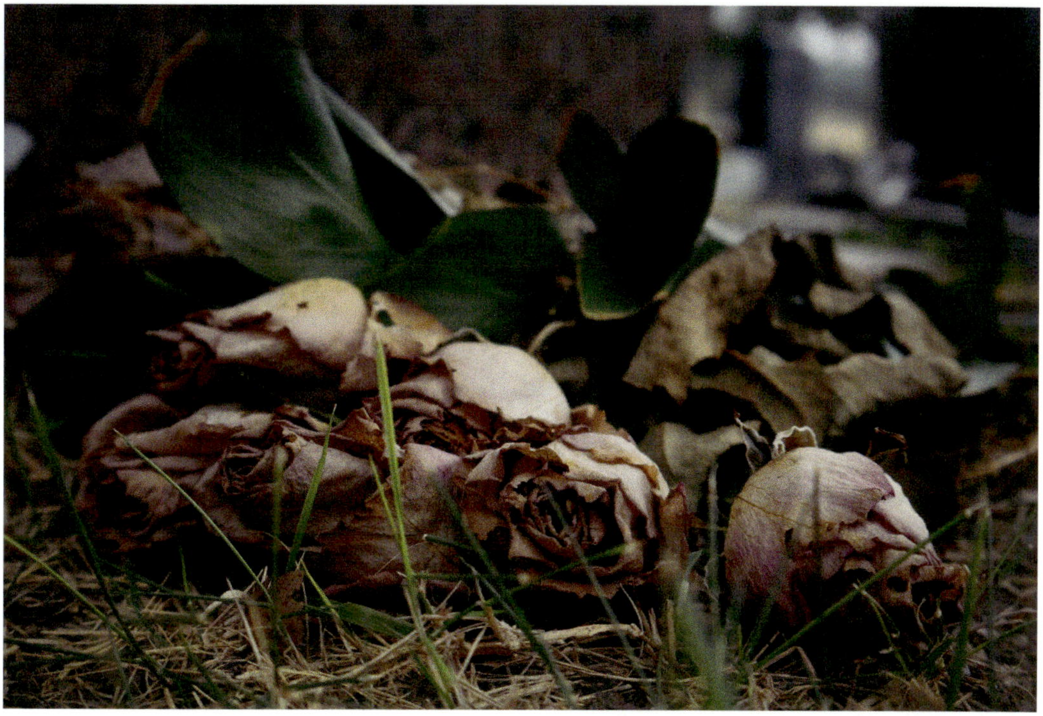

Above : A close-up of a cluster of withered roses lying on the ground, their once-vibrant petals now curled, dry, and tinged with decay.

Right: An eroded cherub, its features softened by decay, becomes a resting place for a delicate harvestman. Nature reclaims what was once meant to be eternal.

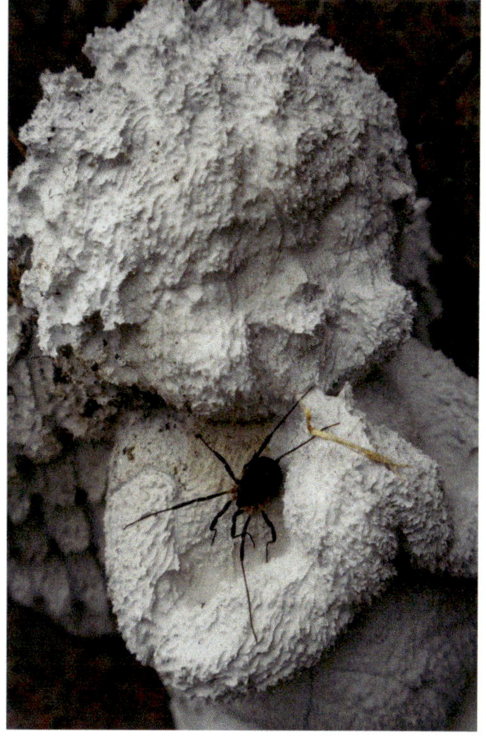

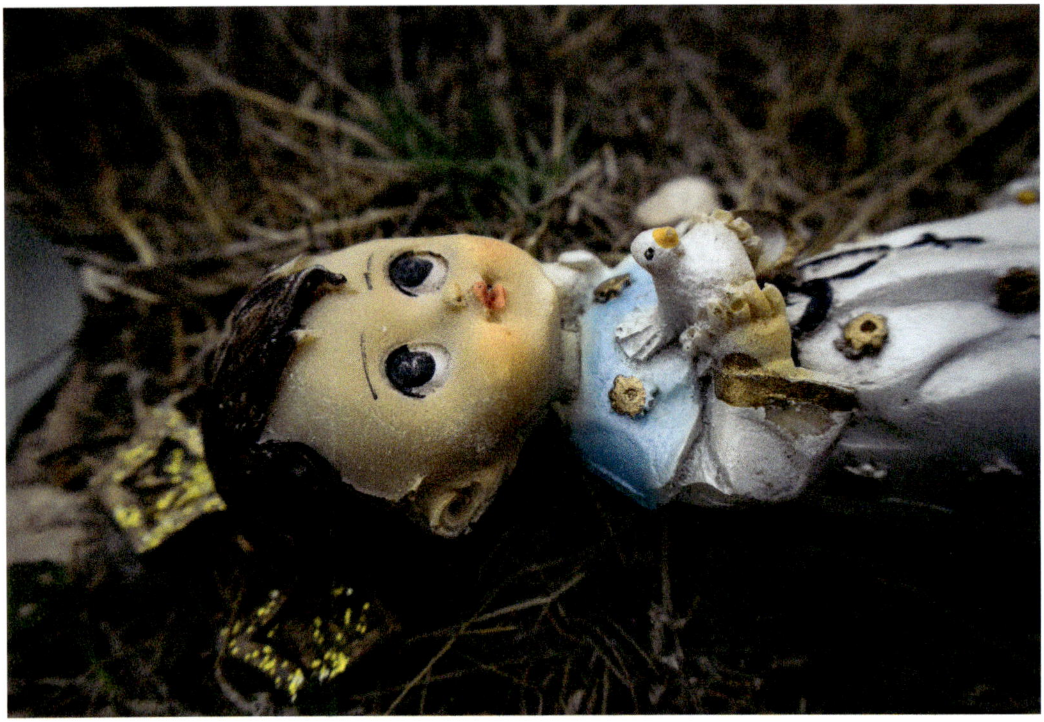

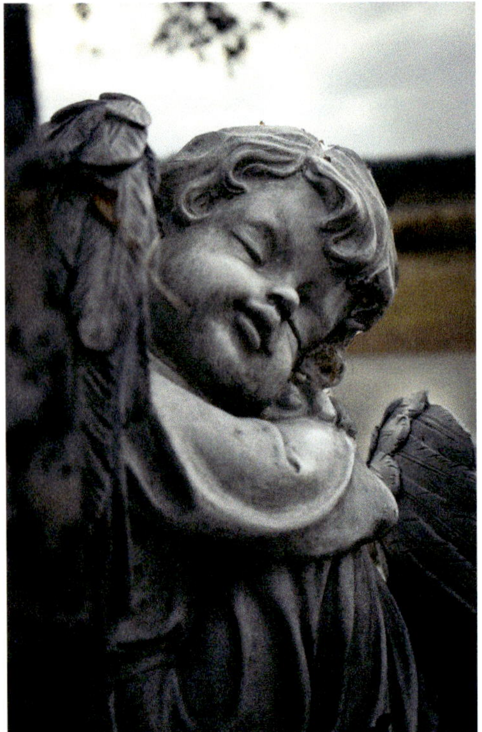

Above: Once a delicate tribute, this statue has succumbed to time, its painted features fading, its surface cracked and chipped.

Left: A serene angel rests in peaceful slumber.

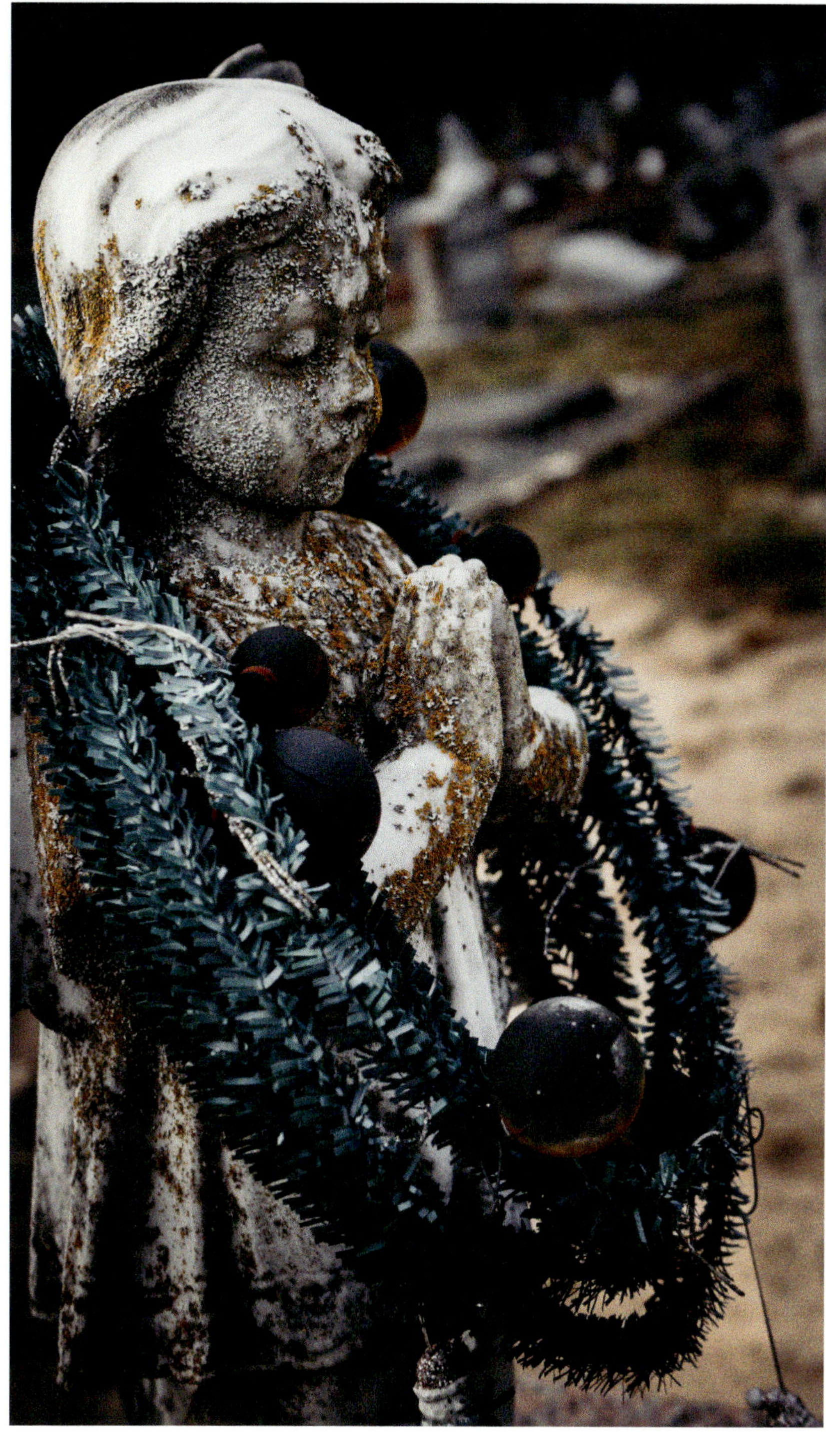

An angel, hands folded in eternal prayer, adorned with faded tinsel and broken ornaments, forgotten yet still standing, whispering silent prayers into the wind.

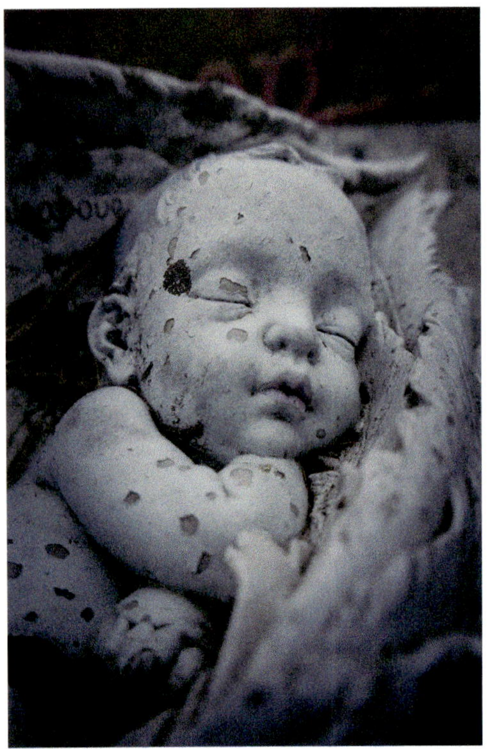

Left: A delicate stone figure lies in peaceful repose.

Below: A small angel sits atop a textured pedestal, holding an open book.

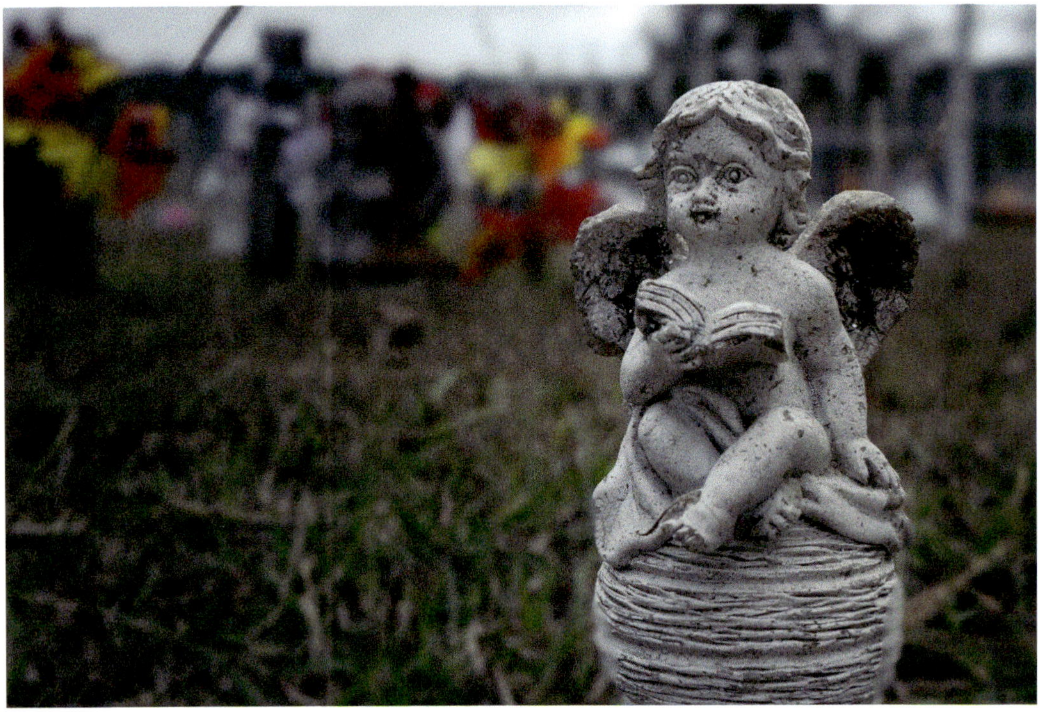

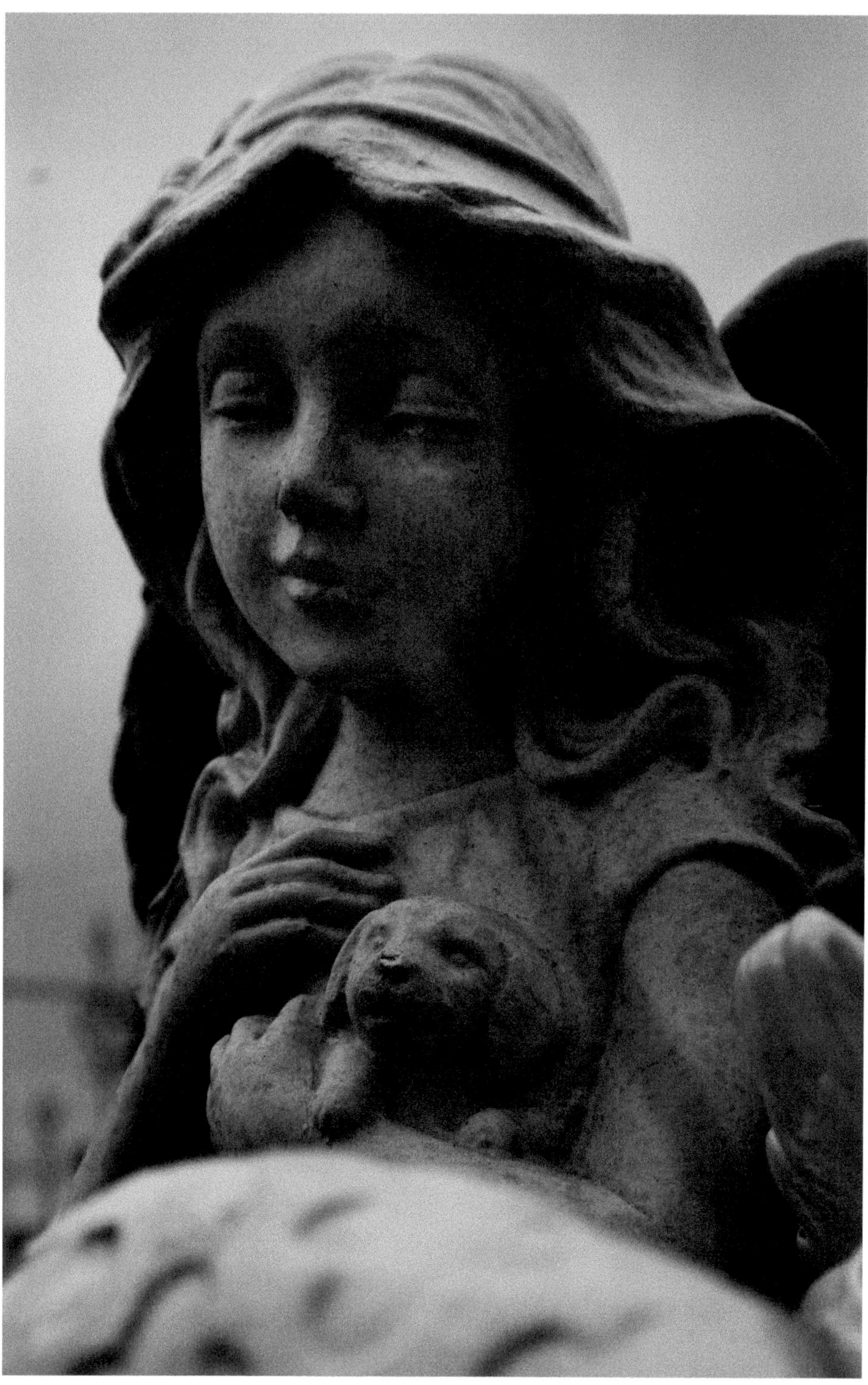

An angel cradles a small dog in her arms, a symbol of eternal guardianship and love.

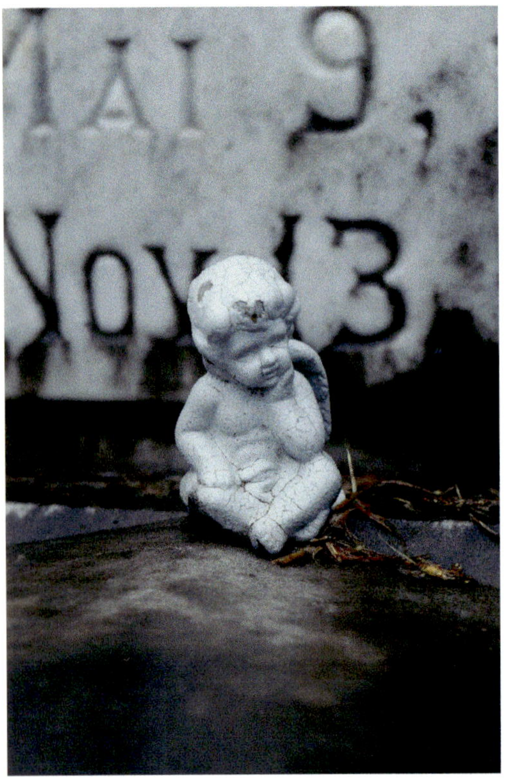

Left: A small, weathered figurine sitting solemnly on a gravestone.

Below: Partially sunken into the overgrown grass, this stone cherub rests in a solemn pose.

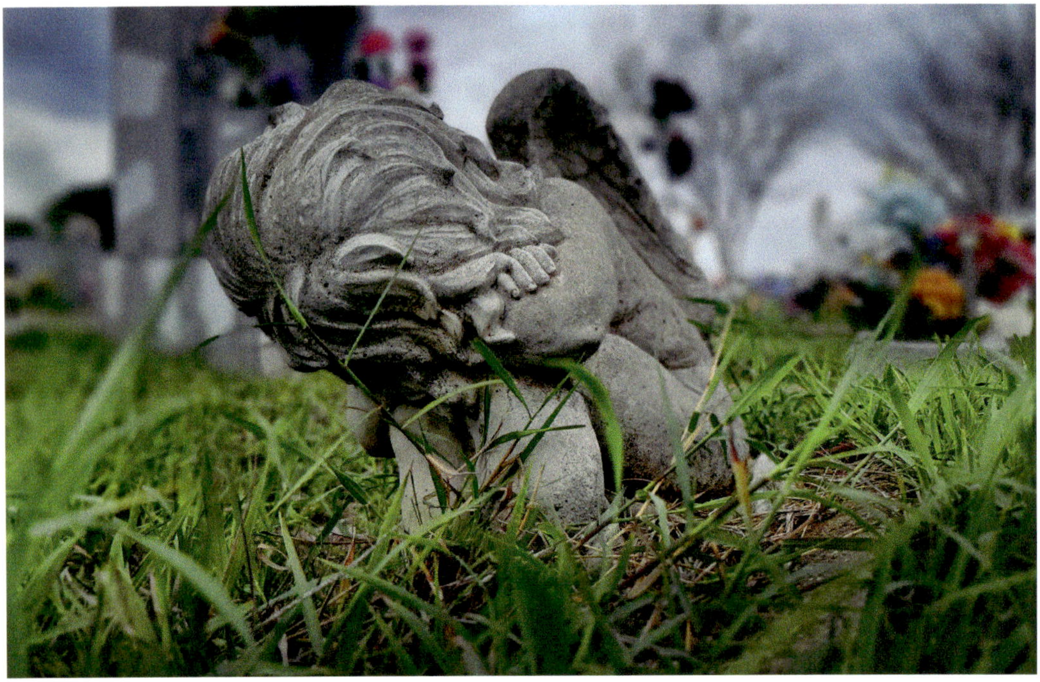

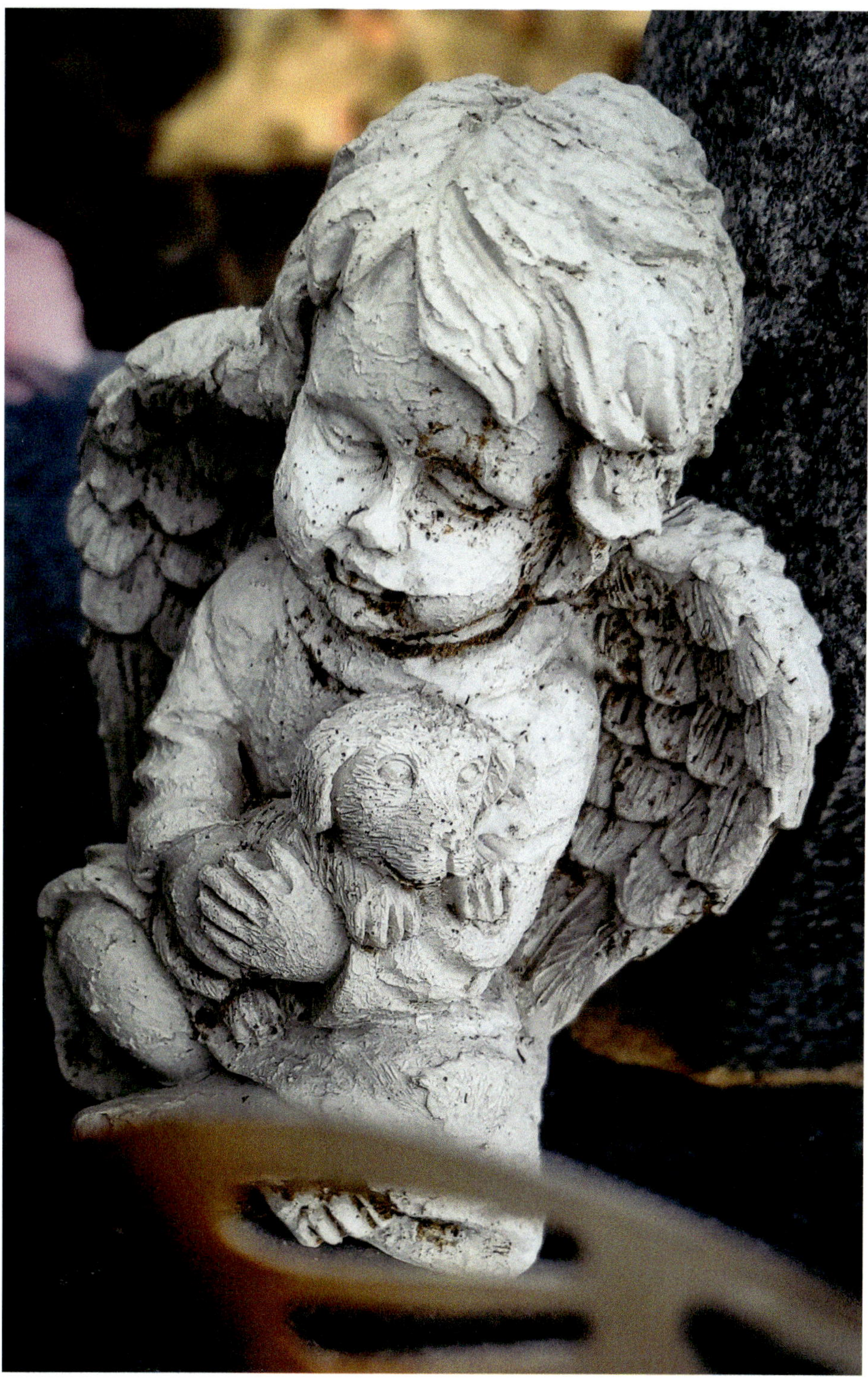

An angel cradles a loyal companion.

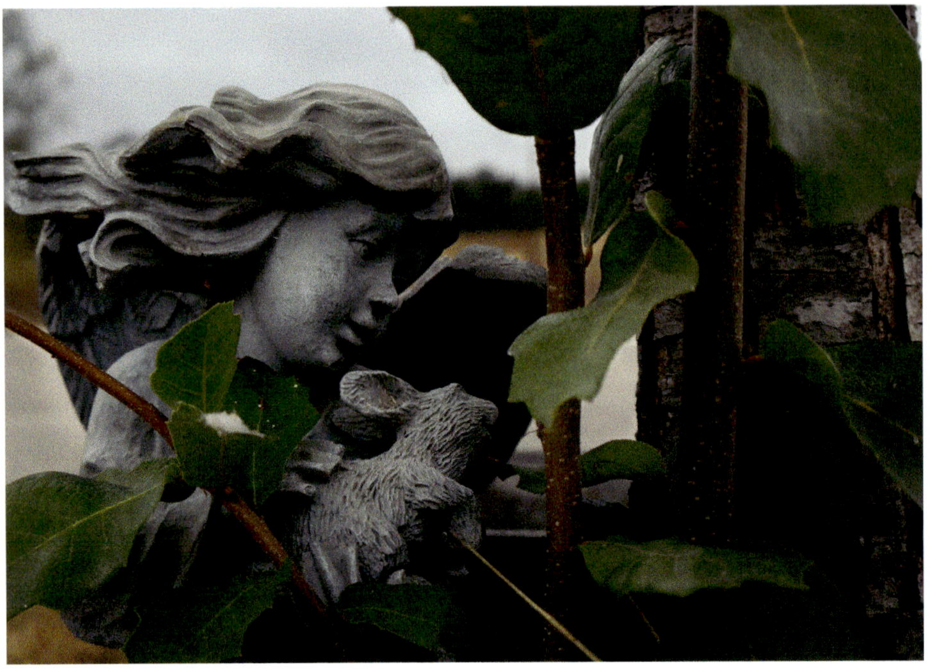

Embraced by time and nature, a gentle angel cradles a lamb.

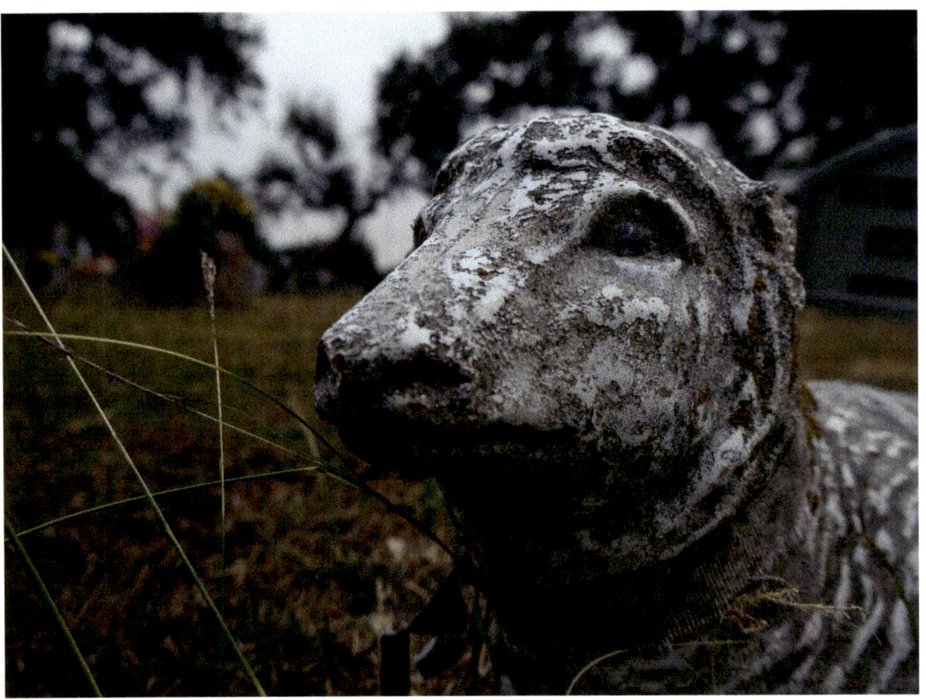

A stone lamb stands in solemn watch over the graves, a silent sentinel of remembrance.

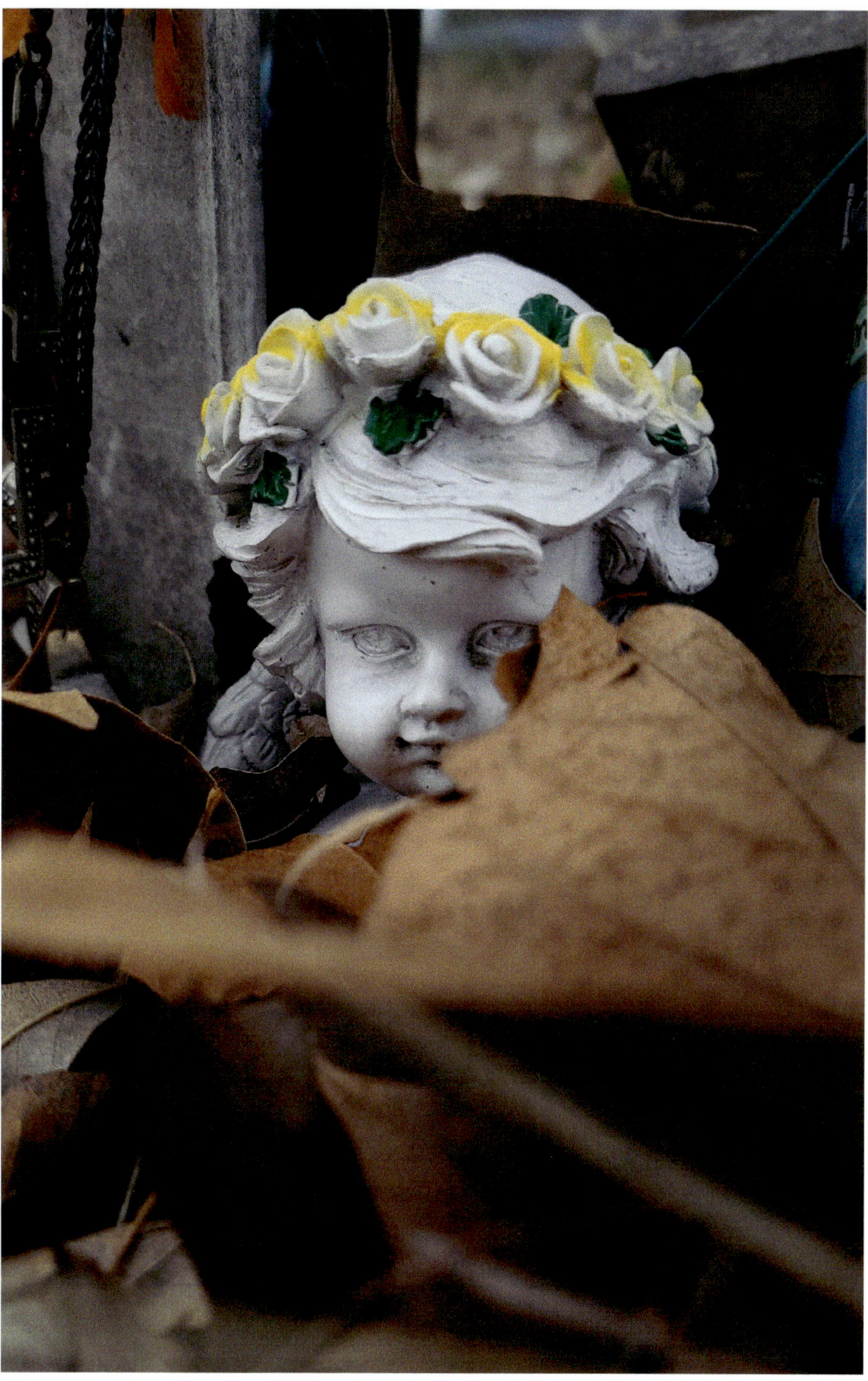

A partially buried cherub statue gazes out from beneath a blanket of dry, fallen leaves.

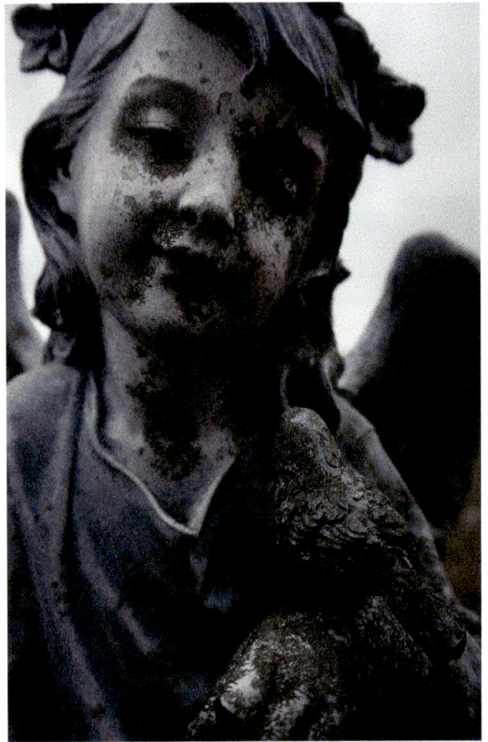

This angel, displaying a faint smile, holds a small bird in its hand.

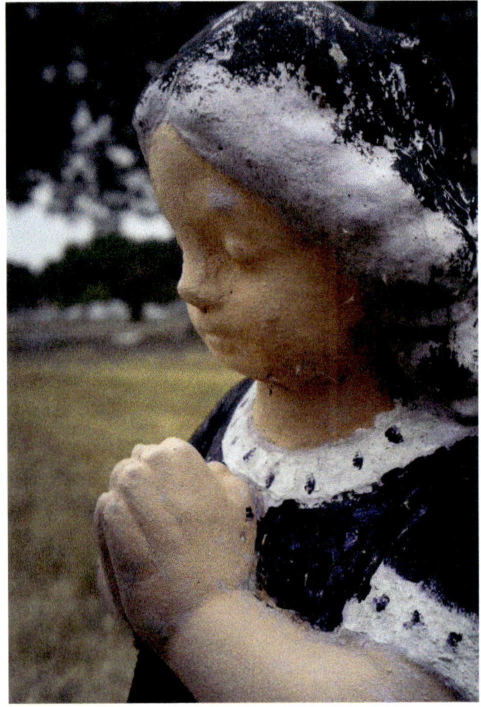

Faded by time, a praying child stands in quiet devotion.

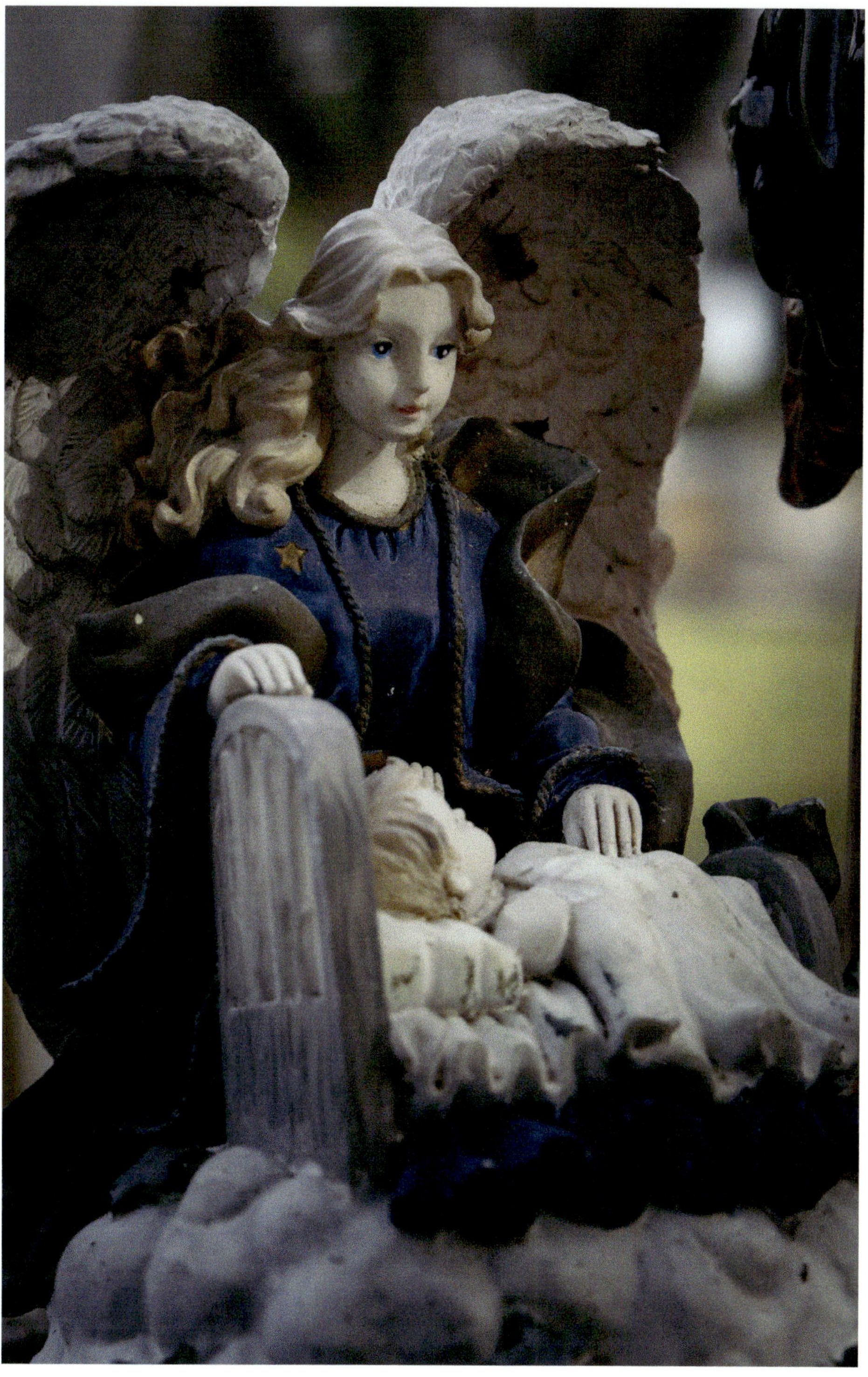

A guardian angel watches over a sleeping child, a symbol of eternal love and protection.

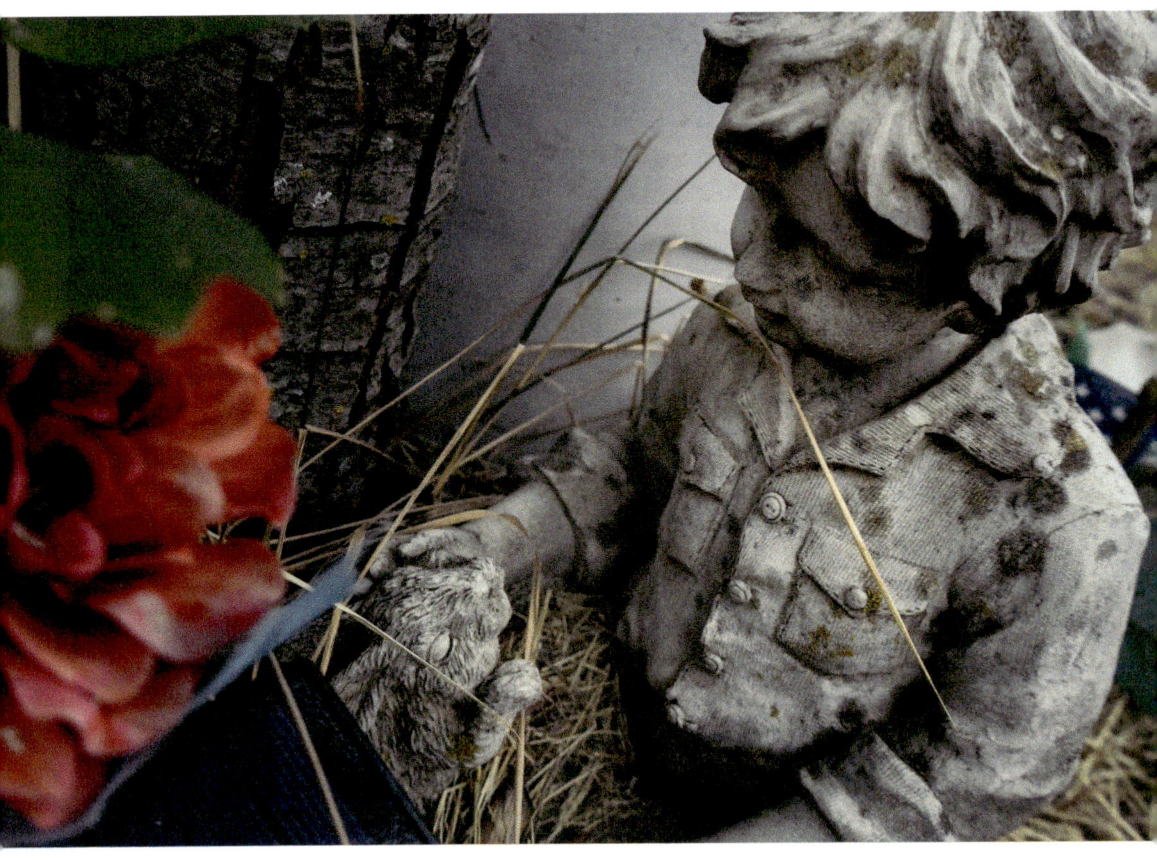

A stone statue of a child kneels in quiet contemplation, gently petting a small animal at their side.

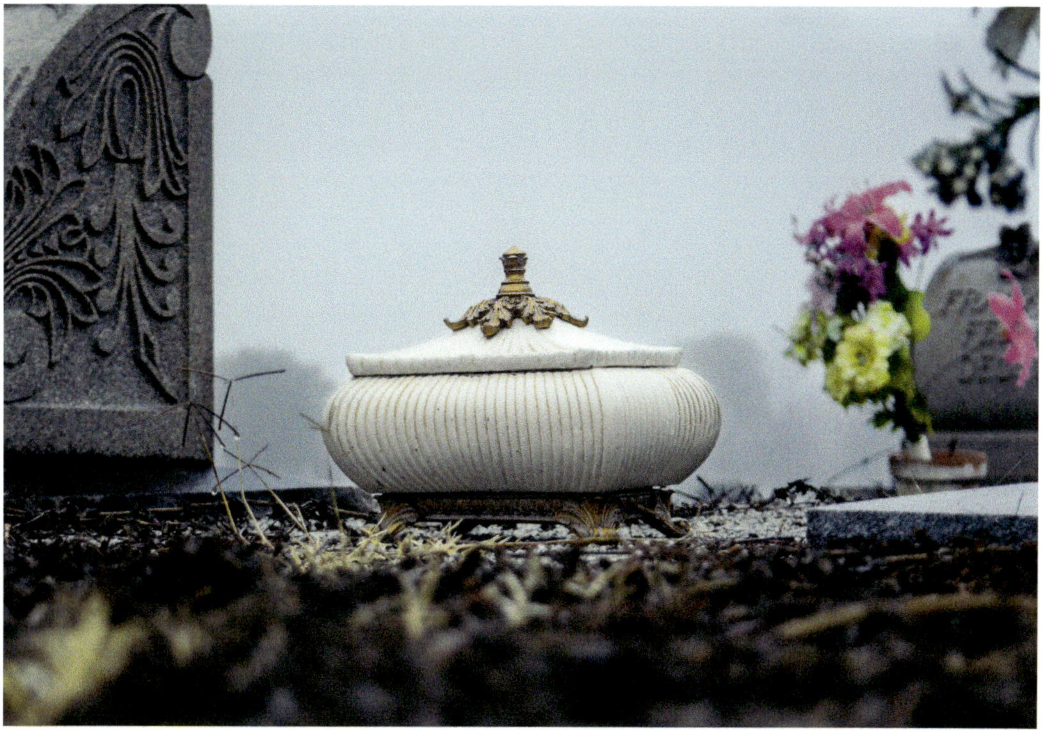

This solemn image captures an ornate urn resting atop a grave.

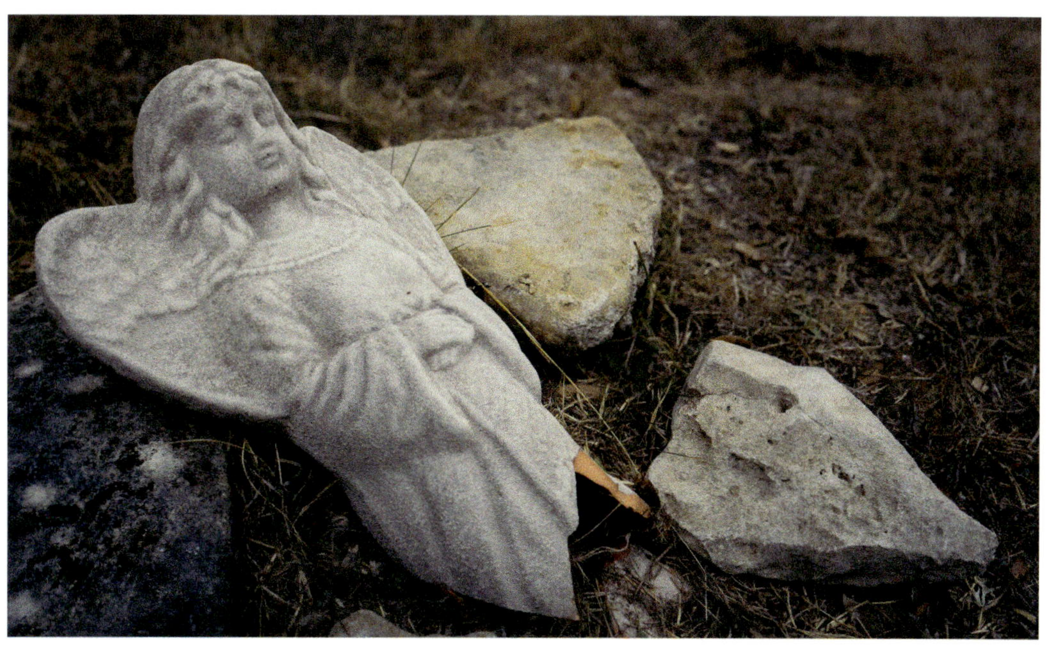

Once standing tall in grace, this angel now lies fallen, cradled by the elements.

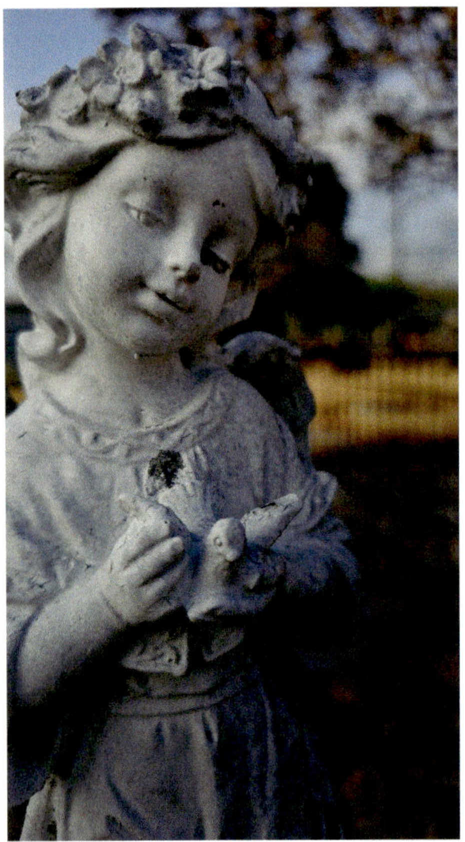

Left: This delicate angel with an expression of gentle kindness, softly closed lips, and half-lowered eyes, looks as if caught in a quiet moment of contemplation.

Below: A grieving angel, its hands gently covering its face in sorrow. The poignant pose evokes a deep sense of mourning and loss.

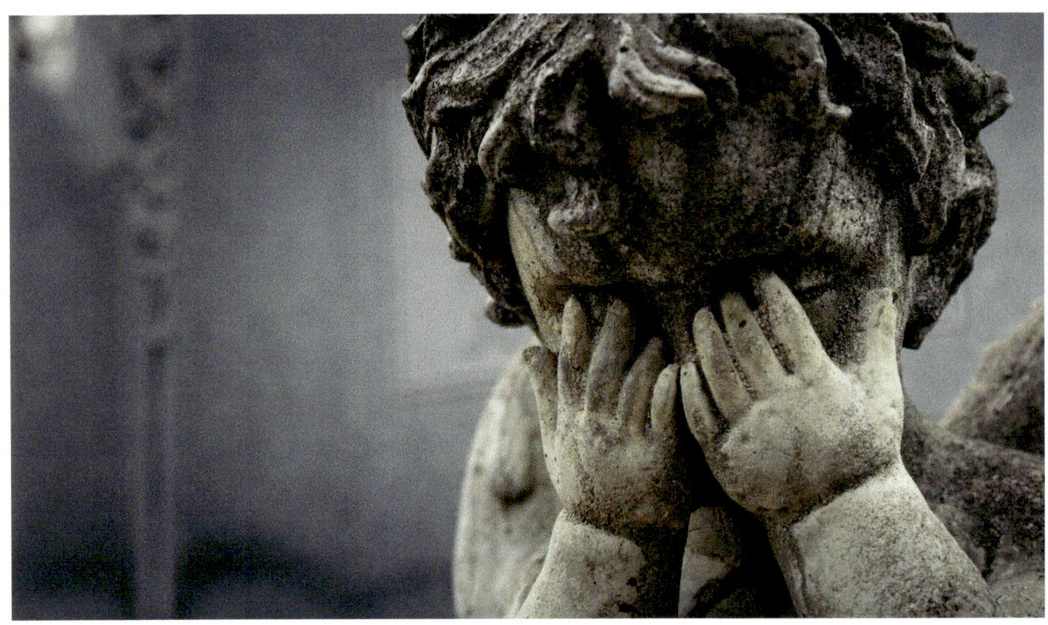